Be aware!
Power and responsibility in the field of sign language interpreting

*Proceedings of the 20th efsli Conference
Vienna, Austria, 14th-16th September 2012*

Edited by

Beppie van den Bogaerde
Liivi Hollman
Marinella Salami

European Forum of Sign Language Interpreters
2013

ISBN 9789081306546

© European Forum of Sign Language Interpreters, 2013

Edited by: Beppie van den Bogaerde, Liivi Hollman, Marinella Salami
Cover design: Triin Jõeveer
Cover photo: Xenia Dürr
Printed by: *Createspace*

This publication is made possible with the support of the EU Lifelong Learning Programme.

All rights reserved
No part of this publication may be produced, stored in a retrieval system or transmitted in any form or any means (electronic, photocopying, recording or otherwise), without the prior written permission of the publisher.

Table of contents

Foreword by Marinella Salami, efsli president 4

Foreword by Beppie van den Bogaerde, editor 6

Power and Responsibility in interpreting situations: The views of Austrian Deaf customers 10
Patricia Brück

(Deaf) Interpreters on television: Challenging power and responsibility 25
Maartje de Meulder and Isabelle Heyerick

Power management – what sign language interpreters can learn? 35
Zane Hema

Interpreting Decisions and Power: Legal Discourse or Legal Discord 45
Debra Russell and Risa Shaw

Identity issues in Sign Language Interpreting 59
Flora Savvalidou

Issues of power and responsibilities in sign language interpreting within sign language users' communities 74
Patricia Shores Hermann

The Power of the profession, taken for granted? 86
Ingeborg Skaten

Abstracts 96

About the contributors 99

FOREWORD

Marinella Salami

"We are made wise not by the recollection of our past but by the responsibility for our future".
George Bernard Shaw

The 2012 efsli Conference was held in Vienna, Austria, from 15th to 16th September, hosted by ÖGSDV (Österreichischer Gebardensprach DolmetscherInnen Verband) – the Austrian Association of Sign Language Interpreters. Every efsli conference has always been a special event for our community. Together with General Assemblies, conferences are efsli's annual gatherings where professionals from all over Europe – and worldwide – meet up again to share achievements, developments, new projects and high hopes within our field.

The 2012 efsli Conference had something more to offer as it marked efsli's 20th anniversary. Not only a moment of celebration that we will indeed cherish and remember forever, but even more a moment of shared responsibility for the future of our profession together with consumers, training institutions and other stakeholders. Not by chance the theme of the conference was "Power and Responsibility". A theme including high values and a wide scope of meanings now collected in this volume. We looked back and we analysed our present. We looked forward with interest and willingness to do more and better. The upcoming years will tell us if the path that we have taken was the right one to follow. Knowing that a road very often leads to other outlets, if we widen our perspective.

The conference was a success and numbers proved it. More than 260 participants from thirty different countries; six plenary presentations, three parallel sessions and poster presentations.

I would like to express my sincere thanks to all presenters and participants for joining us in Vienna and giving prestige to the efsli conference. My gratitude to the ÖGSDV organising committee and all volunteers for their wonderful work and commitment. And thank you efsli: best wishes for the next twenty years of development and improvement.

Marinella Salami – efsli president

Introduction

Beppie van den Bogaerde

This volume comprises seven papers that were presented at the efsli Annual Conference in Vienna, Austria from 14th-16th September 2012.

With a view to the special occasion of efsli celebrating its 20th anniversary, the subjects Power and Responsibility were well chosen. After 20 years of interpreting professionalism in Europe, reflection on the status of sign language interpreters (SLIs) and their influence on the interactions of the people they work for in the different languages is urgently needed in times of change in the Deaf *and* hearing communities. The link between research and practice needs to be tightened to support the changing dynamics in the tripartite communication between deaf and hearing consumer(s) and interpreters and that is exactly what we saw at the 2012 Conference.

The authors, each in their own way, all pay attention to new insights into these changes and bring forth discussions of what the new knowledge actually implies for the interpreting professional. These insights may come from deaf or hearing consumers or from practising SLIs, and are brought forward through different techniques and methods. But all papers contribute to a deeper knowledge about our profession and pave the way for new research, and thus to good, and ultimately best, practice in the field.

Below follows a brief summary of the seven chapters in these proceedings. For a comprehensive impression of the efsli 2012 conference, two abstracts of the presentations that were not submitted to these proceedings are included here as well.

Patricia Brück focussed on power imbalances in interpreting situations by interviewing 21 Deaf consumers. She asked them about their perceptions and awareness of power and responsibilities between/amongst Deaf consumers and hearing interpreters, and about strategies of empowerment use by Deaf clients. The level of education of the Deaf participants was shown to be of importance in the evaluation of power and responsibilities of themselves and of the SLIs.

Maartje de Meulder and Isabelle Heyerick chose one particular sign language situation, viz. television, to argue that television broadcasts are pre-eminently suitable to empower the Deaf community. They list and discuss nine dimensions, which elegantly show that empowering Deaf sign language users to take ownership of their language, not only will benefit the Deaf community, but can also lead to reciprocal learning opportunities both for the Deaf and for the hearing sign language interpreters.

Zane Hema delves into health care settings and based the discussion during his workshop on two papers on *power management* and on *power dynamics*. The participants were asked four questions about their practice in the light of these two concepts. The two studies that were used by Hema provide a fruitful basis for further future discussions, the issues that need to be addressed are a) there is an apparent controversy between accuracy in interpreting and rapport building between doctors, patients and SLIs and b) what should we do to avoid power imbalances in favour of sign language interpreters.

In their paper **Debra Russell and Risa Shaw** look into the decision-making processes of SLIs that contribute to the power dynamics in legal settings. Through an online survey and via focus groups they come to three major determinants, viz. power and privilege and a sense of agency; conceptualising the task of interpreting and training. Across these themes they see that building respectful and professional relationships amongst all participants supports effective interpreting and effective decision-making.

Flora Savvalidou used the framework of the Identity Theory model to investigate the representation of identities in interpreted situations. She explored the relations between SLI's anxiety and their self-talk to identify the power and responsibility that this representation entails.

Her research points to the need of awareness on identity issues for all professionals involved in the sign language interpreting field.

The aim of the paper by **Patty Shores** is to contribute to a better understanding of how the issues of power and responsibilities in SL interpreting emerge, as well as to address the questions of when and why interpreters use power in their professional settings. Moreover, there is a necessity in updating the use of the term 'power' in signed languages to match the current best practices within the sign language interpreting field. By presenting 10 mind-sets, Shores highlights the aspects that play a significant role in establishing power status within sign language user communities.

Ingeborg Skaten goes back to basics in her paper by questioning what actually constitutes a profession and how external factors influence the profession of sign language interpreters. Sources of change in the 'power' of a profession are expertise, jurisdiction and trust. In discussing these concepts Skaten concludes that within the demands of a changing society, SL interpreters need to be proactive if they want to remain involved in redefining their profession.

A call for further professionalization
These papers and the abstracts at the 2012 efsli Annual Conference underline the importance of staying up to date in the debate about sign language interpreting. Societies are changing increasingly faster, Deaf communities included, and the call for a broader and deeper professionalisation as well as the dissemination of knowledge amongst the Deaf is loud. As professionals, we should take constant care that we do not lose sight of the core business of SL interpreting, namely providing a means for deaf and Deaf people to fully participate in modern society. This means a consistently constant reassessment of our involvement and values and these proceedings contribute to this debate in an important way.

Editing this volume was a great learning experience. I would like to thank Liivi Hollman and Marinella Salami from efsli, with whom I edited the papers. The collaboration was wonderful, fruitful and enjoyable and I hope successful. The readers will be the judges of that last aspect, of course.

I will end with a quote by Friedrich Nietzsche:

"All things are subject to interpretation. Whichever interpretation prevails at a given time is a function of power and not truth."

Beppie van den Bogaerde – editor

Power and Responsibility in Interpreting Situations: The Views of Austrian Deaf customers

Patricia Brück
Austria

Keywords: Power and responsibility, Deaf consumers, Austria

Abstract
This paper presents the results of a research study of 21 Austrian Deaf customers aged from 22 to 51 on their view of power and responsibility in interpreting situations. The results show that most Austrian Deaf consumers are aware of power imbalances in interpreted communications (18), that they have been disempowered by the lack of competence of their interpreters, by the lack of interpreters and by their hearing interlocutor. Some 50% of the Deaf consumers - those with secondary education - are aware of their power over the interlocutor and the interpreter; they documents—how they exert it and what measures they take to maximize their power. The paper also discusses the power of interpreters over deaf customers as well as their mutual responsibilities.

1. Introduction

In order to get a picture of the situation of sign language interpreting in Austria, it is necessary to offer some background information on the Austrian Deaf and SLI communities.

1.1 Deaf Education

Austria is a small country with 8,000,000 inhabitants and a Deaf community of about 10,000 people. They are not evenly distributed over Austria, about 25% live in the capital of Vienna where they find the best opportunities for their education and the widest choice of potential professions.

For historical reasons, education for the Deaf has been given mostly in special Schools for the Deaf or hard-of-hearing following the oralist approach that uses only spoken language in class. Upon finishing compulsory school (at the age of 15 or 16), Deaf students' competence of written language is comparable to an 8 year old hearing child. Few of them continue their education and successfully take their A-levels, which would enable them to study at a university (*Zentrum für Gebärdensprache und Hörbehinderten-kommunikation*). Professional education opportunities for Deaf students are scarce and oriented more toward skilled crafts and trades, for which training is offered at schools for the Deaf.

Since 1991, several pilot projects of bilingual classes have been conducted in Klagenfurt, Graz, and Vienna. They have shown that apart from the sign language competence of the teachers, the institutional framework and the composition of the team of teachers are of utmost importance for the project's success.

In recent years, integration of disabled students into mainstream schools has become more and more common. Unfortunately, the state does not provide enough support in sign language to make up for the lack of communication with peers and teachers. The teaching assistants must work in several schools. Each student is entitled to only four hours of support per week (!).

Since the ratification of the UNCRPD (UN Convention on the Rights of People with Disabilities) by the Austrian parliament in 2008, the situation has started to change, albeit at a very slow pace.

1.2 Sign language interpreting

Today, there are about 110 sign language interpreters in the interpreter community in Austria.

Deaf and hard-of-hearing persons are entitled to sign language interpreters in their professional life. They may use them for team meetings, to further their education, for customer meetings and the like. Theoretically, there is no limit; they may use as many interpreting hours as needed. Nevertheless, they have to make formal requests for any interpreting settings that exceed one day (e.g. seminars or training courses).

In contrast, the budget for their private life is strictly limited and amounts from € 2,400 to € 2,600 per year.

Sign language interpreters are used in secondary schools and professional training, but due to the lack of interpreters, not all of these needs can be satisfied. At university level, the GESTU project - *Gehörlos erfolgreich studieren an der Technischen Universität* [Successful Studies for the Deaf at the University of Technology] offers several kinds of services for 13 Deaf and hard-of-hearing students at institutions of higher education in Vienna. GESTU has set up an information centre for Deaf students where information is given in sign language. The project provides tutors, note takers and SLIs for lectures/seminars, conducts research on the use of technical support for the Deaf (remote interpreting, recording of lectures with interpreters) and develops technical vocabulary in various fields where Austrian Sign Language has not yet fully developed. Unfortunately, there is a serious shortage of interpreters, especially for highly specialized settings like university lectures. Therefore, interpreting teams or even a single interpreter cannot be provided for all the lectures/seminars as required by Deaf students.

Although the number of sign language interpreters is growing slowly, densely populated areas like Vienna still suffer from a lack of qualified interpreters. Deaf consumers have to book interpreters four to six weeks in advance to be sure that they will have interpreters for their assignments.

2. Research Focus

Having worked as a sign language interpreter for more than 10 years now, I have grown increasingly aware of power imbalances in interpreting situations. All the available literature has been authored by interpreters and only very few of them included the views of Deaf customers. So I decided to look into
- the perception of power between/amongst Deaf people and hearing interpreters;
- the awareness of Deaf consumers of *power/responsibility* of their interpreters and of Deaf people themselves;
- the *strategies of empowerment* used by Deaf people in interpreted interactions.

3. Study design

The study was conducted among 21 Deaf consumers, 11 women and 10 men, aged 22 to 51 years. Seven of them were from Vienna where 25% of the overall Austrian population lives and 37% to 46% of the Deaf population is located. Another 14 came from four federal provinces (Lower Austria, Styria, Carinthia, Vorarlberg). Due to time and budgetary constraints, it was not possible to find Deaf participants from all nine Austrian federal provinces.

As to their education (see Figure 1), nine participants had undergone professional training, three had completed a trade school, eight had taken High School diplomas and one of them held a university degree.

The data were gathered by interviews conducted in Austrian Sign Language. The 19 questions asked were open-ended questions.
However, I must point out that, because of a miscommunication with one of interviewers, five of the interviewees answered only 15 of the 19 questions.

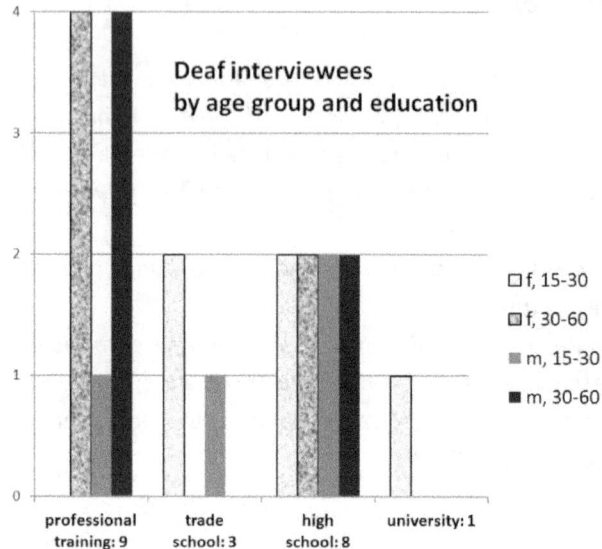

Figure 1

The results were organized in tables, the answers were classified and tagged. The results were evaluated and the occurrences of similar items were tallied.

4. Results

For each of the interview questions presented I would like to use quotes from the interviewees' answers; these are presented in italics below. I chose those that seemed the most representative ones.

4.1 Power imbalances in interpreting? Who has the power?

I would say most of the power is with the hearing person, second is the SLI and the Deaf person is last.

Out of the 21 Deaf consumers, 18 reported to have felt power imbalances, two had not realized any and one person did not know who in the interpreting setting had the most power, six mentioned the hearing person and the hearing interpreter, three thought that the interpreter was the most powerful, four answered that the hearing interlocutor and the Deaf consumer were the ones who had power, one mentioned the Deaf person and four thought that it depended on the situation.

4.2 Disempowerment of the Deaf person? By whom/what?

If the SLI has not got enough education or background knowledge of the topic/situation, I do not get the full information or it may be confused. In such a case I refuse to ask questions, because I know that she will use a lower register when voicing my message.

Twenty Deaf consumers were convinced that they were disempowered; only one of them did not think so.

The most important factor mentioned was the interpreter's lack of interpreting skills (10) (cf. Brown Kurz & Caldwell Langer, 2004:22). Nine thought that it was the hearing interlocutor who disempowered them, four Deaf consumers mentioned that the lack of sign language interpreters was a barrier to their self-fulfilment, four reported that they were disempowered by the interpreting process itself (lag time, information loss, presence of a third person) (cf. Brown Kurz & Caldwell Langer, 2004:19, 42), and four mentioned the behaviour of the sign language interpreter.

4.3 Do you have power? How do you exercise it over the SLI?

I used a SLI for the first time at the age of 15. I did not know who had the power, until I realized it was me. I am the interlocutor of the hearing, the SLI is only interpreting.

Only 10 Deaf consumers out of 16 said that they had power in interpreted communication, two felt they had no power at all, three felt powerful at times and one said that s/he did not know. I think that this result shows that there is much to be done about this problem in the future.

When asked in what way they had power over the interpreter, six interviewees mentioned the physical position of the interpreter and four the choice of interpreter. Another four said that they arranged the appointment themselves (they felt that this alone already gave them power over the interpreter!). Four mentioned that they signed without regard to the interpreter which indicated their trust in the interpreter's skills, four mentioned that they provide information about the setting to the interpreter before the appointment. Not all items that were mentioned are listed, rather only those that were mentioned most often.

4.4 How do you exercise power over the hearing interlocutor?

If I am the customer and have a self-reliant attitude, I can exercise power if my SLI is able to relay it. Power comes from my role and my education, my knowledge, self-esteem and self-reliance.

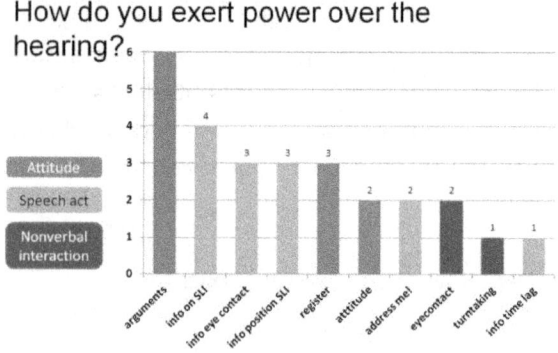

Figure 2

As you can see in Figure 2, six of the 21 consumers think that they can exert power over the hearing interlocutor by using solid arguments to convince them. Four think that they can influence the situation by showing expertise when informing the hearing interlocutor about sign language interpreting; three when informing about the need for eye contact with the interpreter and not so much with the hearing person and about the placement of the interpreter. I find it interesting that most Deaf customers believe that attitude is what most influences the hearing person most (arguments, register, behaviour in the situation), speech acts that show expertise (information on SLI, on shifting eye contact, positioning, time lag, addressing the Deaf person directly) are rated second; only two items were mentioned that refer to nonverbal interaction (eye contact per se, turn taking). I have experienced that Deaf people tend to underestimate the power of nonverbal signals on hearing people.

4.5 How do you maximise power?

If I have to give a speech, [...] I talk about how I want to have my signs interpreted into German (word choice!), ask if the SLI wants the technical terms to be finger spelt or if she prefers to use an intermediate sign that we define beforehand. I inform her about my preferences as to register and word choice (e.g. instead of 'change' pls. use 'modify').

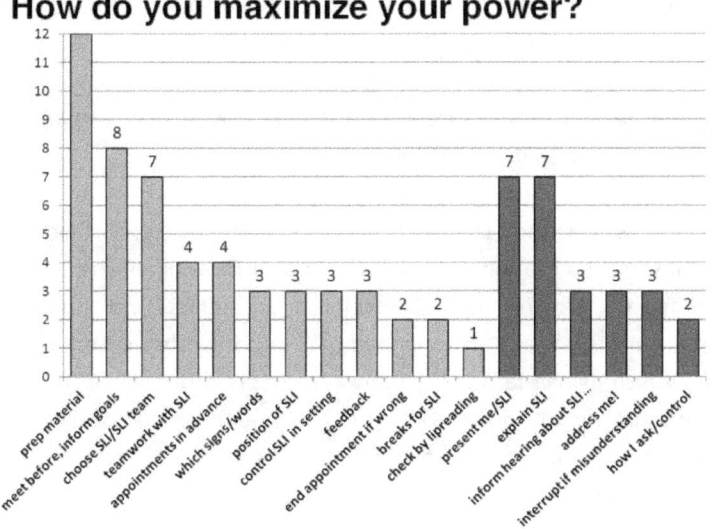

Figure 3

When asked how they maximise power in the conversation (see Figure 3), Deaf consumers mentioned preparation material (12), meeting the SLI before the assignment and informing them about their goals (8), carefully choosing the SLI/SLI teams (7) and other criteria that can be found in the graph above. All these strategies are involving the SLI (dark bars). It is interesting that only few of these tactics aim at monitoring the production of the interpreter (control SLI in the setting (3), check by lip reading (1)). Most of these are team working strategies which I find most promising. Among the strategies aimed towards the hearing person are presentation of the Deaf and the interpreter, the Deaf clients' informing her/himself about SLI (7) and informing the hearing about SLI beforehand (3), asking for recognition as the interlocutor (address me! (3)), interrupting the dialog if s/he feels to have or been misunderstood. Only two interviewees answered that they maximise power by asking questions and controlling the conversation in this way.

4.6 Does the SLI have power? What kind of power?

The SLI exercises power by giving more preference to the hearing person than to my input and not giving me her voice (I cannot shout to make the speaker aware of my input).

When asked if the interpreter had power, 14 respondents answered yes, two said no, and five did not know.

The power of the SLI was to interpret faithfully (5), to take turns (4), to interpret emotions (4), to ask for clarification if she has not understood (cf. Brown Kurz & Caldwell Langer, 2004:27), to choose the right register (4), to take an assignment (2) (among other criteria). I was very surprised by the fact that so few consumers thought of the power of the interpreter to refuse assignments, although several of them had complained about feeling disempowered by the lack of interpreters.

4.7 Do you have power over the SLI outside of the setting? How?

I talk about interpreters to other Deaf people.
As the Deaf community is so small, bad news travels fast - it spreads like oil on water.

When asked if they had power over the SLI outside the interpreting setting, 14 respondents answered yes, six answered no and one person did not know. As to how they had power, six mentioned that they talked about SLIs in the Deaf community, five answered that they would not give an assignment to an interpreter with whom they were dissatisfied, three mentioned that they would provide feedback and three said that they had influence over the SLI by their private contact.

4.8 Does the SLI have power over you outside of the setting?

If there is no personal relationship, they have no power, but if so, their power is huge. I try to have personal relationships with only a few whom I trust and get along with. If there is personal relationship, their moral power is huge, there may be an impact on the relationship if problems in interpreting spill over to our private relationship and the other way round.

When asked if the SLI had power over Deaf consumers outside of the setting, 11 consumers answered yes, nine said no, and one person did not know.

When asked of the kind of influence, they mentioned personal relationships (6), the SLI's influence on their clients' opinion (4), the SLI's choice of assignment (2), choice of the time of assignment (2) and one person mentioned that interpreters may well talk about deaf consumers amongst each other. That only one person mentioned this was a surprise to me, I had expected this aspect to be mentioned more often.

4.9 Do you have responsibilities? Which ones?

I observe the reactions of the hearing person to see if s/he has understood and I ask for clarification, if I something is unclear to me.

When asked for their responsibilities, one person said that s/he did not know about these. The other respondents mentioned 17 items, many of these aiming at the SLI (preparation material (10), organising work breaks (4), signing clearly in order to be understood by the SLI (3), seeing to the SLI's fee (3)), only few aiming at the hearing interlocutor (informing her/him about sign language interpreting (6) and some referring to her/his self-control (control of the situation (4), arranging the appointment (3)).

4.10 Does the SLI have responsibilities? Which ones?

The interpreter's responsibility is also to support the deaf person and even out some of the power differential - her role is that of a cultural mediator.

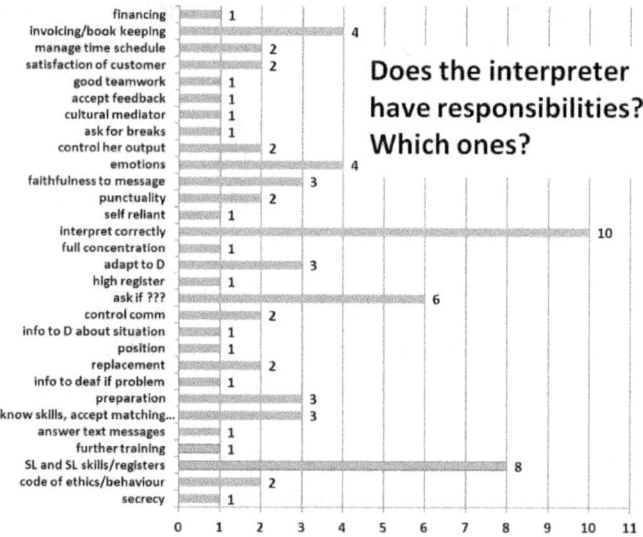

Figure 4

Figure 4 shows that all respondents were convinced that the interpreter has responsibilities. Of the 28 items mentioned, the following scored highest: interpreting correctly (10), having good SL and SLI skills and having many registers in both languages at her disposal (8), asking if the SLI has not understood something (6), interpreting emotions (4) and invoicing and book keeping (4).

5. Conclusion

In general, the results show that Deaf consumers who have received secondary or more education are aware of power imbalances in interpreted situations. They often feel disempowered by the hearing interlocutor and the interpreter, many feel the interpreters' lack of interpreting skills to be a problem.

Only half of the respondents have the feeling of power in the setting, not even a third believe they are in a position to influence the hearing interlocutor by arguments. Most of the strategies used to maximise power are aimed at co-working with the SLI. Two thirds of the respondents think that they have power over the interpreter outside the setting.

Two third of the respondents believe that the SLI has power in the setting, only half of them think that SLIs have power over them outside of the setting.

They believe that they have responsibilities toward the SLI and the hearing person, but they are more concentrated on team working with the interpreter than with the hearing person.

Deaf consumers think that the SLI has a lot of responsibilities. Most of the items mentioned refer to interpreting and quality of interpretation (emotions, registers, etc.).

What I found interesting was the fact that many more Deaf consumers thought they had power over SLIs by talking about them to other Deaf people than they thought of interpreters talking amongst each other about Deaf consumers. I think that they trust in our compliance to the Code of Ethics.

In general my respondents and I have experienced problems with the concepts "power", "responsibility", and "trust". They are blurred and sometimes overlapping so that it is hard to define their boundaries.

I am convinced that we need to work co-operate more closely with our customers to improve the quality of our work and meet their goals more accurately. A lot of exchange will have to be needed in order to find more common ground to help interpreters make more informed choices. Because, as one interviewee put it: *An interpreter has to take decisions all the time!*

References

Anderson, R. B. (1976). Perspectives on the Role of Interpreter. In R.W. Brislin (Ed.), *Translation: Applications and Research*, pp. 208-28. New York: Gardner Press.

Brown Kurz, K. & Caldwell Langer, E. (2004). Student Perspectives on Educational Interpreting: Twenty Deaf and Hard of Hearing Students Offer Insights and Suggestions. In E. Winston (Ed.), *Educational Interpreting: How It Can Succeed*, pp. 9-47. Washington, D.C.: Gallaudet University Press.

Cartwright, B. E. (2009). *Encounters with Reality – 1,001 Interpreter Scenarios*. Alexandria, VA: RID Press.

Clare, K. S. (2000). Recognizing our Humanness. Minimising the impact of interpreting on our professional and personal selves. Paper presented at the AUSIT 13th National Annual General Meeting, Jill Blewett Memorial Lecture, Saturday 4th November 2000, Lennons Hotel, Brisbane.

Kurz, I. (1989). Conference Interpreting: User Expectations. In D.L. Hammond (Ed.), *Coming of Age: Proceedings of the 30th Annual Conference of the American Translators Association*, pp. 143-8. Medford, New Jersey: Learned Information.

Marschark, M., Sapere, P., Convertino, C., & Seewagen, R. (2005). Access to postsecondary education through sign language interpreting. *Journal of deaf studies and deaf education*, (10/1), 38-50.

Mindess, A. (2006). *Reading between the Signs: Intercultural Communication for Sign Language Interpreters*. London: Nicholas Braele Publishing.

Napier, J. & Barker, R. (2004). Access to university interpreting: Expectations and preferences of deaf students. *Journal of Deaf Studies and Deaf Education*, 228-238.

Napier, J., Locker McKee, R. & Goswell, D. (2006). *Sign language interpreting: Theory and practice in Australia and New Zealand*. Sydney: The Federation Press.

Roy, C. B. (1993). The Problem with Definitions, Descriptions and the Role Metaphors of Interpreters. *Journal of Interpretation*, 127-154.

Roy, C. B. (2000). *Interpreting as a Discourse Process*. New York: Oxford University Press.

Seal, B. C. (1998). *Best Practices in Educational Interpreting*. Boston: Allyn & Bacon.

Tate, G. and G. H. Turner (2001). The Code and the Culture: Sign Language Interpreting – In Search of the New Breed's Ethics. In F. J. Harrington & G. H. Turner (Eds.), *Interpreting Interpreting*, pp. 53-66. New York, Oxford: Oxford University Press.

Turner, G. H. (2001). Rights and Responsibilities: The Relationship between Deaf People and Interpreters. In F. J. Harrington & G. H. Turner (Eds.), *Interpreting Interpreting*, pp 22-33. Douglas McLean.

Turner, G. H. (2004). Professionalisation of interpreting with the community: Refining the model. In C. Wadensjö, B. Englund Dimitrova & A.-L. Nilsson, *The critical link 4: Professionalisation of interpreting in the community*, pp. 181-192. Selected papers from the 4th International Conference on Interpreting in Legal, Health and Social Service Settings, Stockholm, Sweden, 20-23 May 2004, John Benjamins Publishing Company.

Wadensjö, C. (1993/2002). The Double Role of a Dialogue Interpreter. In F. Pöchhacker & M. Shlesinger (Eds.), *The Interpreting Studies Reader*, pp. 354-370. Routledge Language Readers. London and New York: Routledge.

Wadensjö, C. (1998). *Interpreting As Interaction*. Harlow, UK: Addison Wesley Longman.

Zentrum für Gebärdensprache und Hörbehindertenkommunikation (Universität Klagenfurt), Kurzinformation über Gehörlosigkeit, http://www.uni-klu.ac.at/zgh/bilder/Folder.pdf. Retrieved September 2012.

(Deaf) Interpreters on television: Challenging power and responsibility

Maartje De Meulder[1]
University of Jyväskylä, Finland

Isabelle Heyerick
Flemish Sign Language interpreter

Keywords: Deaf interpreters, interpreting on television, in-vision interpreting, sign language broadcasting, interpreter training

Abstract

The paper focuses on one particular working domain of sign language interpreters: sign language broadcasting, more specifically television. We will first outline the emerging profession of Deaf interpreters and what they exactly do in which situations. After having explained the difference between sight interpreting and sight translating, we will argue why Deaf people with the appropriate skills and attitudes can and should work as interpreters on television, based on nine different dimensions. We will conclude with some future challenges linked to the training of interpreters and the issue of power and responsibility both within interpreters, the Deaf community and the broadcasters themselves.

1. Introduction

Sign language interpreters find themselves in a continuously evolving profession. Dynamics in society, the Deaf community and the interpreting domain pose challenges and create opportunities. The emergence of Deaf interpreters (DIs) is one evolution in the interpreting profession. Based on our presentation at the efsli 2012 conference in

---

[1] A more comprehensive version of this paper was published in Meurant et al. (2013).

Vienna, the current paper addresses one particular working domain of sign language interpreters: television. We argue why interpreting on television could be considered a 'Deaf job', based on nine different dimensions.

2. Sign language interpreters

For years people working in or with the Deaf community have been accustomed to the term "sign language interpreter" or in some cases the more old-fashioned "interpreter for the Deaf". These labels imply hearing professionals who are trained to interpret in a bi-modal and bi-directional way: spoken language – signed language. In general these interpreters will work in different settings such as community-based settings (social services), in education, in a judicial context and at conferences.

Recently, in Flanders a new working domain has emerged for sign language interpreters: television. This new development is paralleled by the emergence of sign language interpreters who are Deaf themselves. The term "Deaf interpreter" (DI) became widely used when talking about a Deaf person who interprets from a signed language to a signed language, or as is the case for in-vision DIs working from a written text into a signed text through a teleprompter.

Conventionally translating and interpreting are considered two interdisciplinary domains belonging to a general field of study but requiring specific skills, working form different source texts (written versus oral) and demonstrating different processes (interpretation versus translation) (Pöchhacker, 2007; Chesterman, 2004; Gile, 2004). This leads to the assumption that Deaf people working on television should be called translators instead of interpreters, arguing that the source text is in a written form, provided through a teleprompter. However, this conclusion does not account for the *process* that occurs when a DI works from a teleprompter, but only values the modality of the source text. Rathmann (2011) exemplified in his presentation at the efsli 2011 conference that the process that occurs when presenting a written text in sign language on television can be analysed as an *interpreting* process using Gile's effort model[2] (2009).

Based on this theoretical framework, Rathmann distinguishes two modes concerning the conversion of a written text into a signed text. The first one he calls "teleprompter-based" and is used in visual media (TV, websites, e-books). The other one is a "paper-based" mode and can be applied when converting written documents (e.g. state documents) into sign language. Following Rathmann, the first mode leads to (simultaneous) sight interpreting, while the paper-based mode can be termed sight translating. Sight interpreting entails the different phases of simultaneous interpreting, i.e. the interpreter reads and analyses the source (written) text while memory and production efforts are taking place and he/she needs to coordinate these processes in order to be able to take in new information. Moreover, the interpreter has no control over the pace in which the source text is rendered. Except for the usual lag time, the output cannot be delayed and is delivered simultaneously. When considering sight translating, the processes involved are those of a translation effort. The input is a written text as well, but is at all times available to the translator, who can allocate more or less effort to the reading and analysing process. The production process can be delayed in time and can be monitored both during the process and afterwards. Taking into account the process and efforts that take place and not (solely) the source text, we opt to call Deaf signers working on television and other settings where the process entails all

---

[2] Gile (2009) distinguishes three efforts in simultaneous interpreting: (1) efforts in listening and analysing; (2) efforts related to production; (3) the short-term memory efforts. All these efforts must be co-ordinated according to the available capacity of the interpreter.

phases of simultaneous interpreting, as described above, "Deaf interpreters"[3]

3. Deaf interpreters on television

Deaf people taking on interpreting roles is nothing new. What *is* new is that with the emergence of DIs on television, this role has become public. Stone (2005) and Duncan (1997) mention that since the emergence of DIs working on television, there has been a lot of debate about whether hearing interpreters (HIs) should work on television at all or whether this should be primarily "Deaf jobs". Flanders is no exception. The emergence of Flemish DIs in the visual media and especially on television has spurred a lot of debate, both within the Deaf community and within the HI community.

During our presentation at the efsli 2012 conference, we proposed nine different dimensions why Deaf people with the right skills and attitude can and should work as interpreters on television.

1. Practical dimension
With some simple adjustments to working arrangements (e.g. providing an autocue, video footage and access to the script beforehand), Deaf people *can* work as interpreters on television.

---

[3] The authors would like to stress that it is very uncommon to define an interpreter based on audiological parameters (i.e. being deaf or hearing) and not on the interpreters' working languages. Moreover, some of the characteristics of interpreters we will mention in this article are rather due to the interpreter being a L1 or L2 language user than to the interpreter being Deaf or hearing. At the same time, we concur with Stone (2009), that some features of the Deaf Translation Norm are related to the visual biology and cultural aspects of being Deaf. The "Deaf" in "Deaf interpreter" can thus refer to a cultural attribute instead of a mere hearing status. Since Deaf interpreter has become a widespread term, we will not cause any confusion by introducing a new label, but we are aware of and interested in the on-going discussions about this label.

2. Political dimension

Because Deaf people can do it, this adds a political dimension to the situation: these can be said to be "Deaf jobs" (Stone, 2009: 100). HIs should evaluate their role since they are already in high demand in the community where DIs are not always able to work. Another angle to this dimension is that Deaf people expect to be involved in producing the services they consume (Duncan, 1997: 39).

3. Empowerment dimension

By employing a Deaf person to interpret on television, this person acts as a role model for other Deaf people (Stone, 2005: 234) and their environment (hearing parents, family, friends, etc.). An in-vision DI shows another possibility of what Deaf people can achieve, moreover since professional interpreting has traditionally been a hearing position.

4. Cultural dimension

DIs are cultural insiders. Good DIs have the ability to think as other Deaf people think, relying primarily on a visual experience of the world and visual conceptualisation of information (Stone, 2009:167). They are geared to the minds of the viewers (Duncan, 1997:35). This "sameness" and cultural identification is an important factor in establishing rapport and effective communication (Boudreault, 2005: 335).

5. Responsibility dimension

We posit that because Deaf people are members of and live in the minority community they interpret for, it can be argued that they have a different awareness of the responsibility they carry when interpreting, than HIs. Most HIs do not live in the community and as a result do not always see and feel the consequences of their interpreting performance.

6. Linguistic dimension

Apart from the self-evident fact that good DIs need to have (near-) native fluency, there is more to this dimension. Stone (2009) found that the five DIs[4] in his research produce better cohesion, make different use of eye gaze, affirmation, negation and prosodic features, maximise the use of the shared cognitive environment (by incorporating visual information available from the video footage), incorporate enrichments and impoverishments into the target language (TL) to minimise the effort on the Deaf audience, and make use of re-ordering of information to produce an appropriate TL. His research also showed that DIs use a participant perspective, constructing the action or dialogue as if involved in the scene rather than external to it, while HIs use a more detached, observer perspective. Moreover, Stone (2009: 167) posits that DIs are able to produce a "domesticated" TL text that does not look like a translation, giving the audience the opportunity to focus on the information rather than the interpreter. This all contributes to lesser effort on the part of the Deaf audience.

Stone (2009:93) further points out that the fact that the sign language has to fit into the mainstream programme and the absence of mutual adjustment (the HI needs to follow the speed of the hearing newsreader) can be a trap for HIs due to several factors: the complexity of the SL, lack of skills in the TL, lack of mastery of the sign language register or overreliance on certain structures that are thought to be culturally Deaf, but whose overuse identify the interpreter as a L2 sign language user. We further observe that many (Flemish) HIs do not master many subtleties of sign language, which is why they sometimes make mistakes with respect to cultural Deaf norms and values[5],

---

[4] The informants were five Deaf Translators/Interpreters who regularly work within the media, presenting news footage live from English (via autocue) to BSL. They are between 40 and 50 years old, have between four and ten years of experience, and all work in the same geographical area. They all come from Deaf families and have BSL as their first and native language; they would all consider themselves to be culturally Deaf; and they have meta-awareness of the task they are undertaking, including knowledge of the linguistics of BSL from formal education and work at the university level (Stone, 2009).

[5] Some signs can be judged inappropriate in certain situations or when used with certain signers. One example is the sign for breast, which has several lexical variants. One demonstrates the shape of a woman's breast, whereas the other is a more neutral flat hand shape located on the breast. The first variant is

increasing the level of difficulty in understanding them and leading the Deaf audience to reject their performance. Two out of the three interpreter training programmes in Flanders are on the vocational level with limited (i.e. not full-time) contact hours. The third programme established in 2008 is a full-time Bachelor programme in Applied Linguistics with a possibility to pursue a Master in Interpreting[6] where students are trained in interpreting between three languages (Dutch, a foreign main language and a third additional language) and can opt for Flemish Sign Language (VGT) as a third language. Since these programmes in Flanders are facing their own limitations (limited contact hours, financial constraints and institutional prescriptions) they are not (yet) achieving the level of language acquisition one would expect of an educational programme training interpreters for simultaneous interpreting in a wide variety of contexts[7]. Therefore it is to be anticipated that professional L2 interpreters do not fully master all subtleties of VGT.

7. Language ownership dimension

This dimension is about who should be role-modelling sign language within the public sphere and about the need to see one's own language presented by native users of that language[8] (Kyle, 2007:4). By not gatekeeping[9] these jobs, HIs give the Deaf community the opportunity to

---

considered inappropriate when talking about medical situations or in an all-female group of signers.

[6] The MA in Flemish Sign Language (VGT) interpreting was founded in 2008 at the Lessius Hogeschool in Antwerp.

[7] Traditionally the expected level of students starting any interpreter training would be a B1 level (cf. CEFR) in the foreign language(s) and a C1 level (cf. CEFR) of the mother tongue. The two vocational programmes for VGT interpreters state that the achieved level upon completion is a B1 to B1+ level. The MA training at Lessius University was established in 2008 and too few students have graduated up to now to assess the students' language skills according to the CEFR (personal communication with Myriam Vermeerbergen, 19/07/12).

[8] Which Deaf people seem to estimate as a much higher priority than most hearing-run organisations (like public broadcasters) (Kyle 2007).

[9] The notion "gatekeeping" was established in communication research in the early 1950's by David Manning White. The metaphor refers to the complex route of news texts from the original producer to the end user. Vuorinen (1997)

play a core role in publicly showing its language to the mainstream community (Stone 2009:100). Also it is claimed that the development of the language[10] is the responsibility of the Deaf community (Duncan, 1997:38).

8. Process/modality dimension

The way the source text is delivered to DIs is different from HIs, leading to a different outcome. The modality a DI works in is written text to signed production, whereas a HI receives the input in an auditory-vocal manner. This implies DIs do not receive any prosodic elements added by the speaker (pace, rhythm, intonation, etc.). Stone (2009:170) claims this reduces the influence of mainstream culture on the TL and enables DIs to create a Deaf-centred TL (within the confines of the hearing institution). He states this is one of the fundamental aspects of a Deaf Translation Norm.

9. Motivation dimension

While we do not aim to generalize, our experience in Flanders has taught us that most HIs' motivation to work for television seems to stem from the idea that HIs can (and should) help Deaf people acquiring equal rights through access to information. This is made clear in statements the HI applicants expressed when asked what their motivation is to become in-vision interpreters: "Deaf people have the right to the same information as hearing people", "I want to help Deaf people to gain their human right to information". This motivation differed from the DI applicants' motivation, who tend to foreground the empowering and linguistic aspect; "acting as a role model", "working to L1", "making television accessible for deaf children who can't read subtitles", "news in own language".

---

defines it as the process of controlling the flow of information into and through communication channels. She applies the notion to research translated news items (from English into Finnish) and states: "The gatekeepers decide what messages or which pieces of information shall go through a particular gate and continue their journey in the channel and what not ("in" or "out" choices), and in what form and substance these messages are allowed to pass."

[10] E.g. coining new signs, choosing which signs to use, grammar etc.

4. Conclusion

While DIs have always been around, it is only recently they have become visible in Flanders, especially at conferences and as interpreters on television. This stirred the debate both within and between public broadcasters, the Deaf community and interpreter community about what DIs do, and when and why DIs are needed. Traditionally DIs are requested in conventional settings or for certain consumers when a HI feels s/he cannot adequately do the job. Interpreting on television is rarely mentioned as a possible professional domain for DIs and more often than not, HIs feel they can adequately do this job.

In the UK and recently in Flanders it has become clear that television is and should indeed be a working domain for DIs. In this article, we distinguished nine dimensions why Deaf people with the right skills and attitudes can and should work as interpreters on television.

However DIs and HIs are confronted with several aspects leading to certain power issues. We can conclude that some of the issues are caused by the attitude of HIs and DIs, others by lack of awareness in the Deaf community and still other issues because of the views and unawareness of broadcasters.

The future poses challenges, which can hopefully lead to some new opportunities. Whereas the professional situation of DIs and HIs needs to improve, the synergy between interpreters can lead to reciprocal learning opportunities. If the Deaf community takes on these challenges, it will enable them to gain control and real ownership of their language.

References

Boudreault, P. (2005). Deaf interpreters. In T. Janzen (Ed.), *Topics in signed language interpreter: theory and practice,* pp. 323–355. Amsterdam: John Benjamins.

Council of Europe – Language Policy Division (2001). *The Common European Framework of Reference for Languages.* Cambridge

University Press.
Chesterman, A. (2004). Paradigm Problems? In C. Schäffner (Ed.), *Translation Research and Interpreting Research. Tradition, Gaps and Synergies,* pp. 52–56. Clevedon: Multilingual Matters.
Duncan, B. (1997). Deaf people interpreting on television. *Deaf Worlds, 13(3),* 35–39.
Gile, D. (2004). Translation Research versus Interpretation Research: Kinship, Differences and Prospects for Partnership. In C. Schäffner (Ed.), *Translation Research and Interpreting Research. Traditions, Gaps and Synergies,* pp. 10–34. Clevedon: Multilingual Matters.
Gile, D. (2009). *Basic concepts and models for interpreter and translator training.* Benjamins Translation Library Series, vol. 8. Amsterdam: John Benjamins Publishers.
Kyle, J. (2007). *Sign on Television: Analysis of Data. Based on projects carried out by the Deaf Studies Trust 1993-2005.* Bristol: Deaf Studies Trust.
Meurant, L., Sinte, A., Van Herreweghe, M., & Vermeerbergen, M. (2013). *Sign Language Research, Uses and Practices. Crossing Views on Theoretical and Applied Sign Language Linguistics.* Berlin: De Gruyter.
Pöchhacker, F. (2007). Critical linking up: Kinship and convergence in interpreting studies. In C. Wadensjö, B.E. Dimitrova & A. Nilsson (Eds.) *Critical Link 4,* pp. 11–23. Amsterdam: John Benjamins.
Rathmann, C. (2011, September 16) *From Text to Sign: information reception, processing and production.* Presentation at the efsli conference "Sight Translation – Sight Interpreting – Meeting at the Cross Modes", Salerno, Italy.
Stone, C. (2005). Deaf Translators on Television: reconstructing the notion of 'interpreter'. In Meer et al. (Eds.) *Connections 4,* pp. 65–79. University of Bristol.
Stone, C. (2009). *Toward a Deaf Translation Norm.* Gallaudet: Gallaudet University Press.
Vuorinen, E. (1997). News translation as gatekeeping. In M. Snell-Hornby, Z. Jettmarová & K. Kaindl (Eds.), pp. 161–173. John Benjamins: Amsterdam.

Power management – what sign language interpreters can learn?

Zane Hema

Sign Language Interpreter
United Kingdom

Keywords: Power Management, Power, Reconciliation, Facework

Abstract

Fowler defines power as "the ability of people and institutions to control the behaviour and material lives of others". (Fowler 1985:61). In the context of interpreted interaction, do interpreters have the ability to control the behaviour and material lives of others, if so, how is this played out in interpreted interaction? Do interpreters consider the relationships between participants and themselves, if so, how is this played out? In order to answer these questions this paper brings together the findings of two studies looking particularly at healthcare interpreted interaction. The findings were presented to a group of sign language interpreters as a basis to examine and develop current practice.

1. Introduction

The efsli workshop entitled "Power Management – What Sign Language Interpreters Can Learn?" which took place on 15 September 2012 was principally based on two works *Community Interpreting: Re-Conciliation through Power Management* by Merlini & Favaron (2003) and the discussion chapter of an unpublished PhD thesis by George Major entitled *Healthcare Interpreting as Relational Practice* (2013). Using the findings of these two studies, a number of questions were posed to workshop participants. First though it will be helpful:

- to define the words *power (management)* and *reconciliation*;

- to make a number of points about the two studies before giving a summary of their findings;
- to specify the four questions asked;
- to provide a commentary on "Power Management – What Sign Language Interpreters Can Learn?" from the notes of the group discussions.

Merlini & Favaron (2003: 213) define "power (management)" as the *ability of people and institutions to control the behaviour and material lives of others* adding that *power (management) is a skill that can be learned and practised*. The *power* that is managed manifests itself in the context of social interaction (discourse). Merlini & Favaron assert that an interpreter manages the power dynamic in order to secure an outcome that is favourable to the participants. Indeed they define a favourable outcome as a Reconciliation. Their study took place in Melbourne in 2001 and data was collected from 32 healthcare interpreting assignments of 12 NAATI[1] certified interpreters (all female aged 27-60) across a range of medical settings.

Whilst the focus of Merlini & Favaron's study was power management the focus of Major's 2013 study looked at the interpersonal dynamic in healthcare interpreting. Indeed the purpose of her study was to gain a deeper understanding of the dynamics of healthcare interpreted interaction (relationships) and to examine what interpreters are doing. Major was interested in how interpreters deal with the development of rapport between doctors and patients, threats to rapport, and whether or not they engage in facework. More detail on this concept will be provided when the findings of her study are summarised later in this article (see section 3).

For now Major's study looked at two real life recordings where one of the interpreters was related to the patient and the other was not. She also looked at a range of role plays carried out with a General Practitioner (GP) or family doctor. Major's study looked at the work of

---

[1] NAATI – National Accreditation Authority for Translators and Interpreters.

Australian Sign Language (Auslan) interpreters working between Auslan and spoken English whereas Merlini & Favaron studied the work of spoken language interpreters working between Austraitalian (a particular type of Italian spoken in Australia) and spoken English, but both studies focussed on interpreting in healthcare settings.

2. Power management (Merlini & Favoron 2003)

To look at how interpreters were *managing power* to achieve a *favourable outcome,* Merlini & Favaron looked at six areas. These are:

1. *Preparation* – to what extent were the interpreters able to have pre-assignment conversations with either the patient or healthcare professional?
2. *Phonology* – particularly the tone of voice and speech rate of the interpreter.
3. *Lexis* – the lexical choices made by the interpreter.
4. *Divergent renditions* – the extent to which the interpreter would omit, add or change the source language.
5. *Footing* – the interpreter's way of framing their interpretations in relation to the participants present.
6. *Non-verbal features* – the interpreter's use of gestures, their spatial relationship with participants and their use of eye contact.

They found that in terms of 1. *Preparation*: healthcare professionals were more willing to have a preparatory conversation with the interpreter (14/32) than were the patients (2/32). With regard to 2. *Phonology:* accent and loudness of the voice were low relevance indicators. However the interpreters had a more marked tone of voice when addressing the patient than they did when addressing the healthcare professional. Concerning speech rate, interpreters had a faster speech rate with the healthcare professional than they did with the patient. The interpreters stated this was because of their desire to maximise clarity. In the case of 3. *Lexis,* the use of technical jargon was infrequent. There was a higher degree of formality with the healthcare professionals. The interpreters frequently paraphrased English expressions in order to overcome the potential difficulties of obscure terms. Also the interpreters adjusted register when one language was consistently delivered in a less formal register and the other in a formal register where complex explanations are rarely given clearly.

When analysing 4. *Divergent renditions* they found that *additions* were the most common type. The interpreters would check that all was OK (*phatic addition*); or repeat a message (*emphatic addition*); or make an *explanatory addition* in order to seek clarification. This could be to point out that the patient has not understood, even though the rendition was correct or to alert the patient to a missed inference or to provide the required information. There were few *omissions,* indicating that an interpreter may omit a term that could be inferred from context. Regarding *substitutions* interpreters did not depart from the content of the original message. They did make *modifications* to soften remarks that might otherwise cause alarm.

Looking at 5. *Footing*, it was rare to find the healthcare professional or the patient address the interpreter directly. Also interpreters used indirect speech into English even when the healthcare professional had addressed the patient directly. The main finding in terms of 6. *Non-verbal features* was that the patients' visual orientation was towards the interpreter whom they clearly saw as a less threatening figure than the healthcare professional (2003: 225).

The purpose of Merlini & Favaron's study was to investigate what brings about effective communication in a real life cross-cultural interaction, taking place with real people in a real physical environment. What is it about the interpreters' performance that brings about effective communication and most importantly is it a result of the interpreters' (conscious or even unconscious) use of *power management* strategies?

Their findings indicate that interpreters behave in a number of ways in order to bring about effective communication. As shown above, they will slow down their speech rate interpreting to the patient in order to maximise clarity. They will soften remarks that may cause alarm. They will make additions to their interpretations to check comprehension, to seek clarification or to make it known that the patient has not understood the interpretation even though it was an accurate one. Furthermore they will alert the patient to a missed inference or provide the required information on behalf of a participant. In addition to paraphrasing English expressions to avoid confusion of obscure terms, interpreters would be deliberate in their lexical choice in order to reduce the divide in the register of each language.

In summary, interpreters do use *power management* in order to ensure effective communication and to bring about a "favourable outcome" for both the healthcare professional and the patient and if done successfully, a favourable outcome also for the interpreter.

3. Dynamics of healthcare interpreted interaction (Major 2013)

Turning to the second study, the purpose of Major's study as stated above was to gain a deeper understanding of the dynamics of healthcare interpreted interaction (relationships) and to examine what interpreters are doing.

Major was interested in how interpreters dealt with rapport-threatening talk; how interpreters convey the doctor's and the patient's attempt at building rapport; and how then does the interpreter manage their own relationship within the consultation. Major refers to the work of Silverman, Kurtz and Draper (2005) which states that good doctor-patient rapport has been shown to enhance accuracy, efficiency and supportiveness, satisfaction for both patient and doctor, and health outcomes for patients.

Major found that interpreters actively attended to the maintenance of doctor-patient and doctor-patient-interpreter rapport. This was seen in the interpreters conveying the intent of rapport-orientated talk i.e. humour. Also the interpreters engaged personally in rapport-orientated exchanges to a small extent, i.e. smiling or laughing at jokes. They also encouraged doctor-patient rapport by strategically not interpreting during brief moments where doctors and patients were attempting to communicate directly (i.e. through gesture, eye gaze, pointing, etc.).

During rapport-building moments such as social talk and humour, therefore, interpreters would often prioritise these interpersonal moments over accuracy in message equivalence. This prioritisation would see interpreters add, omit, and change information. Major proposes that interpreters should also understand that it is sometimes acceptable to engage to a certain degree in rapport-oriented talk such as small talk and humour. She further suggests that interpreters do *facework* (Goffman, 1967). *Face* is a person's sense of worth, honour and personal value. You can lose *face*, claim *face,* your *face* can be threatened or enhanced. A potentially *face* threatening act can be mitigated and this is what sociolinguists refer to as *facework*.

She found that both interpreters did *facework* by actively toning-down *face*-threatening acts. Occasionally, confrontational utterances were even omitted. Both interpreters influenced the flow of interaction by moving past difficult talk. The interpreter who was related to the patient did this quite overtly, and the other interpreter did it subtly, through the way she managed turns during overlapping talk.

Major looked at interpreters' clarification requests and found that the interpreters in the role-plays were *active agents* in seeking clarification not only for themselves but also in conveying others' clarification requests. She sees *clarification* as a skill interpreters need to master. Interpreters mainly clarified in order to ensure accuracy, for example because they do not understand the *message* or there is a need for repair. However, Major also found that doctors and patients expect interpreters to clarify. That is, interpreters should consider strategically building in clarification requests into their work even if unneeded because of the expectation from the participants.

Major concludes that interpreters are *Powerful Agents* in terms of facilitating good rapport between the doctor, patient and themselves.

Her study also shows in reality interpreters are making decisions not only on linguistic equivalence of a message, but also in order to facilitate good rapport even if this means making changes to the interpreted message. Worthy of note here is that she found that in discussion about medicines, symptoms and diagnoses interpreters were very focussed on accuracy and rapport was less of a priority.

4. The efsli workshop

Conference participants were asked to discuss the following questions in four groups; (a) what is your *aim* when interpreting in the healthcare setting; (b) how relevant are the findings of the two studies to your own experiences; (c) to what extent does your role as the interpreter differ from what you understand you should be doing versus what you do in reality; (d) is there any value in developing a self-analysis tool to enhance practice and if so, what would it look like. Participants were interpreters from all over Europe. The status of Deaf people, recognition of sign language and development of sign language interpreting as a profession varies from country to country. There were approximately 80 participants (average of 20 per group) and discussion time was limited to 90 minutes. The following summarises the groups' responses to the four questions, with quotes presented in italics.

(a) What is your aim when interpreting in the healthcare setting?

In reporting following discussions, participants appreciated that interpreting in healthcare settings can be complex and so they did *not want to make things any more complicated than they already are*. But participants wanted to be *totally sure that the message is clear to the patient and the healthcare professional* and that the patient *makes his/her own decisions*. In terms of power, participants thought one of their aims is *to reduce power imbalance*.

(b) How relevant are the findings of the two studies to your own experiences?

The summaries in (a), (c) and (d) demonstrate relevance to the findings of the two studies. In (a) the desire of an interpreter to maximise clarity is consistent with both studies and in (c) participants see their role as more than just interpreting between two languages; that there is also a need to attend to rapport between the patient and the healthcare professional is again consistent with both studies. Participants agreed that *facework* was a strategy interpreters could use to deal with sensitivity and awkwardness. An example might be seen on decisions they make on the use of the first or third person. One question they asked is whether there is a risk of doing too much *facework*. But from their comments above, the level of *facework* may be determined by the level of sensitivity or awkwardness.

(c) To what extent does your role as the interpreter differ from what you understand you should be doing versus what you do in reality?

Participants all agreed that they clarify to ensure accuracy and maximise clarity. But participants added the need to make explicit who was seeking clarification. Participants also raised the concern of whether an interpreter answering the patients request for clarification make take some responsibility away from the healthcare professional. Participants worked with patients who did not seek clarification and considered it part of their role to encourage the patient to do so because they would have *greater ownership of the situation.*

They agreed that the role of the interpreter should be to facilitate *smooth* communication and this is most effective when there is trust and understanding. This *smooth* communication has respect for the patients' autonomy and self-determination and also ensures that the healthcare professional understands *a bit of deaf culture* and that clarity for the patient is maximised.

Participants saw themselves as gatekeepers and talked about two of their strategies to ensure *smooth* communication. The first was vocalising patients' non-manual features or gestures (in the absence of signs) to serve a particular purpose. More interesting was that some participants thought *taking the blame* for another's misunderstanding was a strategy that helped communication run more smoothly.

Participants' decision-making was influenced by the age/gender of the healthcare professional and the degree to which they modified their language. The status of Deaf people and the level of training vary from country to country and are also influences.

(d) Is there any value in developing a self-analysis tool to enhance practice and if so, what would it look like?

Participants grappled with this question and the discussion probably warranted more time. Participants agreed that it would be useful to have some tool that would serve to provide an analysis of how they managed power or showed examples of them doing *facework*. Initial thoughts came up with the idea of a checklist that an interpreter could take to an assignment. Similar checklists to analyse other aspects of interpreting already exist and so these can be modified. But essentially this would a type of self-assessment.

Participants suggested that the patient and healthcare professional also had some input. Unfortunately the group were unable to expand further on how this would look but since they viewed successful interpreting in the healthcare setting as a collaboration between the patient, the healthcare professional and the interpreter, then any analysis should need to look at the collaboration.

It was agreed that the interpreter should always continue to ask themselves questions about their interpreting and about the decisions they made.

5. In conclusion

There was much value in discussing these two studies, but due to limitations of time there is a need for on-going discussions if not at the European level, then within the context of each country. The two studies provide a valuable framework for on-going discussions. Perhaps discussions could start with two following questions

- If interpreters see accuracy in their work as paramount but at times prioritise rapport building between the patient and the doctor and themselves, what does that mean in understanding the role of the interpreter in reality?
- Merlini & Favaron conclude that interpreters manage power to achieve a favourable outcome, while Major says interpreters are Powerful Agents in terms of facilitating good rapport between the patient and the healthcare professional and the interpreter. Could there be outcomes which are overtly in favour of the interpreter and if so, what would these look like and what precautions are needed to avoid this?

References

Goffman, E. (1967). On face work. In E. Goffman (Ed.), *Interaction ritual: Essays on face to face behaviour*, pp.5-46. New York, NY: Anchor Books.

Major, G. (2013). Healthcare interpreting as relational practice. Unpublished doctoral dissertation. Sydney: Macquarie University.

Merlini, R., & Favaron, R. (2003). Community Interpreting: re-conciliation through Power Management, *The Interpreter's Newsletter*, 12, 205-229.

Silverman, J., Kurtz, S. & Draper, J. (2005). *Skills for Communicating with Patients* (2nd ed.). Milton Keynes Radcliffe Medical Press.

Interpreting Decisions and Power:
Legal Discourse or Legal Discord

Debra Russell, PhD
University of Alberta

Risa Shaw, PhD
Gallaudet University

Keywords: Legal field, decision-making, power dynamics

Abstract

This *efsli 2012* presentation shared preliminary findings of our study of the decisions interpreters make that may contribute to the power dynamics in interpreted interactions in legal settings and with legal discourse. We looked at what elements influence decision-making of very experienced legal interpreters and how these interpreters see the concept of power impacting their work. The data showed interpreter perspectives on the constructs of power, and approaches to dealing with power issues. These issues revolved around three major themes: how interpreters understand the task of interpreting (conceptualization of the task), whether interpreters see themselves as having a sense of agency in their approach to the work, and in their interactions, and the training and support interpreters have in their work in this specialized area. The findings have implications for practitioners and those training interpreters for legal discourse and settings.

1. Introduction

Interpreters working with legal discourse and in legal settings are faced with making choices and decisions that ultimately affect the power dynamics for all involved in the interaction. This paper reports preliminary results of a research study that focused on interpreters who work in a range of legal settings in Canada and the United States. The focus of the research was to investigate interpreter decision-making related to their work and how these interpreters see the concept of power impacting their work. We explored choices made about determining qualifications for assignments, working conditions, working in teams, preparation, and mode of interpretation (consecutive and simultaneous), as well as how participants understand the concepts of power and how the interpreter understands and exercises power in legal interpreting situations. In addition, we explored how working in Deaf and non-deaf teams affects the power dynamics and how these Deaf/non-deaf teams are perceived by legal system personnel.

For the purposes of this study we examined two types of power: the inherent power relationships within the legal system, and the power dynamics within a legal interaction or exchange that involves an interpreter. Within the legal system, for example, the court or prosecutor is in a position of power over a defendant. Within an interpreted interaction, an interpreter may have increased power by virtue of their role, because the participants are relying on mediated communication. When gathering data in the study, we did not provide a definition of "power" for participants; rather we allowed them to describe it in their own ways.

The findings reveal distinct and varied approaches to dealing with power issues and also show that interpreters are aware of their decisions and resulting actions affecting the power dynamics in legal settings. Three major themes emerged in this study: the interpreters' sense of agency; how the interpreters conceptualize the task of interpreting; and how they view the impact of specialized training on their work. The findings also highlighted some of the effective practices experienced interpreters use in order to deal with power issues. What also emerged was evidence of the importance of well-trained Deaf/non-deaf interpreter teams that trust each other to not bring their own power imbalances into the work. While the data is from Canada and the U.S., and is restricted to interpreters dealing with English/ASL, the findings can be compared with other papers presented at the efsli 2012 conference, including the work of Brück, De Meulder & Heyerick, Savvalidou (all found in this volume).

2. Methodology[1]

In this study we were specifically interested in the legal system, which includes court, police interactions, social work interviews, school meetings, lawyer interviews, and other situations that have a legal component. Using a qualitative and ethnographic approach (Bogdan & Biklen, 1992), we selected participants through purposeful sampling to allow for "information-rich cases whose study will illuminate the questions under study" (Patton, 2002: 231). Participants were invited via electronic mail, and were provided with a description of the research project. They then completed a brief on-line survey and were invited to participate in subsequent focus groups. We recruited participants who were nationally known and credentialed Deaf and non-deaf, and CODA[2] interpreters who had over 15 years of experience working in legal settings in Canada and the U.S.

The goal of this qualitative study is to explore the following two questions:
- What decisions do interpreters make that contribute positively or negatively to the power relationships within an interpreted legal interaction and what elements influence their decision-making?
- How do very experienced legal interpreters see the concept of power impacting their work?

The on-line survey had 16 respondents (100% of those invited), which included seven Deaf and nine hearing participants, 50% who grew up in a D/deaf family, 12 females and four males. Data on participant

---

[1] The space constraints of this paper do not allow for a literature review. See Russell and Shaw (in progress) for an in depth discussion of the literature framing this study.
[2] A term used in North America to refer to hearing children of Deaf adults, i.e., native ASL users.

demographics showed the majority of participants had over 20 years of interpreting experience, and over 15 years of interpreting in legal settings.

Fifteen (15) of the 16 respondents agreed to participate in focus groups. We conducted these focus groups using remote video conferencing. Due to timing, 12 people actually attempted to participate in one of three focus groups. However, because of technical difficulties, only nine people were able to participate in the focus groups. Focus group participant demographics included two Deaf and two hearing Canadians, one Deaf and four hearing people from the United States, three non-Caucasian participants, three who grew up in Deaf families, and five who grew up using ASL. The focus groups were conducted in ASL, using the same eight open-ended questions to guide each focus group. Data was recorded through software programs and Quicktime movies were made of each focus group.

The principal researchers and two nationally certified interpreters coded the data using ELAN, drawing on grounded theory approaches to analyse the data. Analysis of qualitative data is a cyclical and reflexive activity requiring data-led, systematic analysis (Coffey & Atkinson, 1996). This methodology is used to "discover important patterns, themes, and interrelationships [which] begins by exploring, then confirming [, and] is guided by analytical principles rather than rules" (Patton, 2002:41).

3. Findings

Three major thematic categories emerged from the data analysis: interpreters' sense of agency, conceptualization of the task of interpreting, and training. Each of the categories and their subthemes are defined and described below. A number of the themes and sub-themes intersect, which we discuss below.

The participants provided numerous examples that demonstrated that when interpreters are aware of their own power and privilege, as interpreters and as individuals, they can chose to make professional decisions that may impact the power dynamics in interactions in appropriate or positive ways. Alternatively, interpreters may misuse their professional and/or personal power. The decisions made are significantly influenced by the power of the legal system, and the roles that participants in that system perform.

3.1 Power and Privilege and a Sense of Agency

Awareness of one's professional and personal power and privilege is a self-reflective exercise that centres on one's sense of agency. The sense of agency construct refers to the subjective awareness that one is initiating, executing, and controlling one's own actions in the world. It reflects a sense of the interpreter being able to exhibit ownership and responsibility as it pertains to their individual decisions and actions in the interpreted interaction.

In this study, the participants' descriptions of their perspectives and actions indicated how a sense of agency or lack of agency allows them to conduct themselves with ease, or experience significant challenges. The sub-themes associated with this category include:
- Awareness of choices
- Recognizing the impact of decisions
- Establishing positive relationships
- Assertiveness
- Being willing to change interpreting practices.

The following quotes in italics from participants reflect an awareness of their own power and privilege in interactions, demonstrate a sense of agency about the interpreting work in terms of forming positive relationships, and recognizing the impact of the interpreter's decision-making:

Over the years I have worked with many people [lawyers, judges, legal personnel] to educate them about interpreting and what is needed.

How I present myself to the legal personnel shapes everything.
In contrast, other participants showed a lack of agency, which also impacts interpretation in a legal setting. For example, the following quotes demonstrate a sense of helplessness to impact the legal system in terms of hiring practices:
Sometimes you can't do any preparation. No one gives you information. There are no documents. The police and the lawyers just keep putting you off. Sometimes the lawyer is willing to take a few minutes with you, but often not.

There are times when I have no say over what a court will or won't do. There's nothing I can do.

3.2 Conceptualizing the Task of Interpreting

Interpreting is a highly complex, cognitively demanding activity (Pöchhacker, 2004; Seleskovitch, 1978; Wadensjö, 1998). Conceptualization of the task refers to one's understanding of the cognitive and practical elements required to produce an accurate interpretation. These elements include:
- Understanding the goals of the participants in the interaction;
- Employing appropriate cognitive processes to produce an interpretation that respects those goals;
- Producing an accurate, linguistically and culturally appropriate interpretation product.

The interpretation must reflect and incorporate the context in which the interaction is occurring. The context of the event will shape the linguistic and interpretation decisions made by the interpreter. Understanding interpreting as a meaning-based activity that presumes participants are working together to create meaning (Wilcox & Shaffer, 2005) implies that the interpreter's task is much more than word-sign equivalency and form-based transcoding.

Throughout the focus groups, the interpreters emphasized the importance of a variety of factors that contribute to more or less effective interpretations: for example, determining whether they are qualified for a given assignment, requiring a specific and qualified team, needing preparation time with participants and materials, taking time to conduct preparation, and determining the mode of interpretation that will allow for the work to be accurate and effective. All of these can be understood as elements of the task of interpreting. The participants discussed the importance of establishing working conditions that allow for their choices and decisions that will shape their ability to interpret effectively.

However, the data showed the interpreters had varied perspectives on how and to what level they are able to achieve these working conditions. From our preliminary analysis of the data, we believe these variations correlate to differences in training, conceptualizing the task of interpreting, and exhibiting agency. For example, an interpreter without appropriate training may accept an assignment without knowing and approving the team composition. This is influenced by how an interpreter see a team working and whether they see that all members of the team are responsible for the entire interpretation, regardless of the roles at any given time (actively producing the interpretation or being the monitor and support interpreter). In turn, the training and understanding of the task impacts the interpreters' sense of agency, or lack thereof.

The following quotes from participants speak to the sub-themes of preparation, specific job requirements of the legal interaction, practices and strategies that support professional and successful team interpreting and effective overall interpretation:

An essential part of doing this work is taking the time that is needed, and not letting myself be rushed. That time is to meet with the parties involved, meet with the other interpreters, and prepare with what resources that exist of that assignment. Respecting the integrity of the work is taking the time that it needs.

One determining factor is who I will be working (teaming) with. We have to be able to work together, or we can't do the job. This includes being able to give and receive feedback from one another, as well as what type of training we have.

Both of these comments represent interpreters demonstrating confidence, taking responsibility for their own work, and creating working contexts that support successful interpretation *in light of how they understand the task of interpreting as a whole*. The non-deaf participants also revealed a heightened awareness of balancing professional power in a team by sharing power with their Deaf colleagues, and using strategies that have the potential to shift legal system perceptions of Deaf people. As one participant said:

I am easily intimidated [in a police situation] so I ask the Certified Deaf Interpreter to take the lead. This decision gives the Deaf interpreter the power and also serves to educate the police officers who can then see the Deaf interpreter as equal. This is a conscious decision of mine.

Interpreters recognize that there are professional standards to be observed, and prioritize their interpreting needs, as is shown in the following quotes:

You have to be able to stand your ground. When you [the hearing interpreter] realize that you cannot go forward without a Deaf interpreter working with you, you have to ensure that one is brought in.

It is important to interpret consecutively because that is best practice, but it is also important to use Consecutive Interpreting (CI) because it is the way to be accurate.

In contrast, another participant reflected a view that knowing the community and courts may absolve one of her/his responsibility to actively prepare for each specific job.

I've worked in my community for 20 years and I know the courts and the people and though sometimes I am surprised, most of the time I know what will happen [and I do not need to prepare].

The following quote stresses the importance of constantly being aware of one's beliefs and views about the work, the consumers for whom we provide service, and the need to adjust practices based on new experiences or information.

I worked a case with a well-educated Deaf person who had a Master's degree from Gallaudet University and who requested a Certified Deaf Interpreter CDI for the court proceedings. [...] My first response was that there had been a mistake and I told the judge it was not my practice to interpret for someone like this. I realize how inappropriate I was to assume I could make the decision for this Deaf person. [...] She said that she wanted a CDI because she wanted full access to the proceedings in her first language, ASL, and she did not want to have to deal with the code-switching the hearing interpreters would produce. I learned a valuable lesson that anyone can benefit from the services of a CDI. And that changed my way of thinking and my practices.

The data also showed a reflection of the power dynamics between some Deaf and non-deaf interpreters, and the misuse of power on the part of the non-deaf interpreters.

The hearing interpreter is the first person assigned, and then I [Deaf interpreter] might get assigned to the job. The hearing interpreter often says they are fine and don't need me there. But they don't necessarily have the ability to assess their own skills for the job. [...] The hearing interpreter will get to the job and realize they do need me. Then I get a last minute call. Deaf interpreters are an afterthought.

When I arrived at court, and I was there intentionally early, the 4 hearing interpreters were already in a meeting with the lawyers. Neither I nor the other Deaf interpreter on the case were invited to join the meeting or brought up to speed on what was being discussed. [...] We were completely left out of the process [because of the hearing interpreters' actions].

3.3 Training

The third broad category that emerged in the data was that of training. Participants discussed the training they had and the need for more, both continuous and specific, in order to do the work in this specialized area of interpreting legal discourse and working in legal settings. The sub-themes in this category include:
- Meaning based interpreting
- Specialized knowledge/practice
- Team practices
- Views of consumers
- Educate consumers

The following quotes represent the need for training that addresses how interpreters conceptualize the task of interpreting and how that impacts the interpreted interactions. These quotes focus on team practices and the misuse of power:

I told the hearing interpreter I needed clarification on something. She refused to get clarification. Then I looked to the second hearing interpreter on the team and she also refused. They both said 'no' they wouldn't get the clarification. I could not believe they said "no". On top of that, everyone in the courtroom was waiting on the interpretation. […] Do I have no say in the interpreting work?

I would like to see agencies implement policies to hire a Deaf/hearing team for all legal jobs. That way they would avoid having hearing interpreters who don't have an accurate assessment of their work, which would avoid [the hearing interpreter making] errors. This all goes back to who has the power to decide who is hired [the agency and/or the hearing interpreter].

The data reveals some contrasting views between Deaf & non-deaf interpreters, specifically related to teamwork and how their views on the task of interpreting differ:

We need to get information from the attorneys and the Deaf person. But I hate when the hearing interpreter oversteps and asks the Deaf person for personal information. You have to know what to ask and not ask, and how to let the Deaf person give what information they want to give.

Hearing interpreters have told me they don't need a DI, and yet those hearing interpreters don't have the judgment to know when a DI is needed. I've been in situations where a DI is needed, but the hearing interpreter doesn't see it.

Deaf interpreters see power dynamics in everything we do – the hearing interpreters sometimes get it, but often don't. Do they understand their own privilege as a dominant society member?

The data showed that interpreters could identify decisions that reflected an awareness of system power and how their own knowledge can be used to create working conditions that support effective interpreting practices.

If you understand the system and how power operates in the legal system, then you can navigate through the system to get what you need.

I know that I can ask that a case get moved on the docket if I have to be somewhere else. It is use of my power that I prefer not to use, but do use sometimes. It's nice of them to make an exception for me, but I think the Deaf person has a right to have the opportunity to fully experience the court proceedings.

As indicated earlier, the focus group participants are from two countries that have had different paths to training. This resulted in some differences that seem to relate to a lack of agency and lack of training in the area of legal interpreting. For example:

I have withdrawn from a case when the interpreting team is not working out. I didn't like what is happening, so I just walked out.

The courts decide who is qualified, so if you are on the list, that is it.

3.4 Intersection: System Power + Power and Privilege

The data revealed examples that highlight the intersections among concepts of power, privilege and interpreters' sense of agency, conceptualization of the task of interpreting, and training. These intersections cut across the power dynamics of concepts of systemic power, power in the legal system, and one's own personal and/or professional power and privilege.

The following quote poignantly represents one example of the intersection of system power and power and privilege:

People have their pre-conceived notions of who I am when I enter the room, regardless of the fact that I am entering in a professional role. Because of that, I go into interpreting situations in a less than powerful position. I am black and because of how other people see me, hold the same power that other professionals hold. [...] So, I must present myself each time, as a consummate professional.

4. Discussion

The participants in this study demonstrated an awareness of power dynamics and of how the constructs of power affect us as individual interpreters, as well as how we as interpreters affect the power dynamic in an interpreted exchange through our conscious and unconscious decisions. The data provided numerous examples of individual or internal factors related to power, in the categories of sense of agency, conceptualization of the task and training. We also uncovered factors that either related to the individual interpreter or a group of interpreters and external contexts that impact the balancing of power and the misuse of power. Finally, there were themes that demonstrate the impact of the greater society in which we live and the institutions with which we interact, that also have a significant influence on the decisions interpreters make and resulting interpreting work. Across all of these themes, we see that building respectful and professional relationships among all participants' supports effective interpreting and effective decision-making, in the immediate and subsequent interactions.

The data set represents the cyclical and recursive nature of making effective decisions that address the power dynamics in the interpreted interactions, and we sense this framework could serve as the possible basis of training, supervision, and mentorship for interpreters in general and training for working in legal specialization. From the data the foundation of effective decisions seems to start with a strong understanding of power and privilege at two levels: societal and personal. From one's personal awareness of power and privilege, one can develop a sense of agency and understanding of power and privilege in interactions. This then is applied to how the interpreter understands what it means to provide effective and accurate interpretation in any context. Ultimately, this is influenced by her interpreter training as a generalist, and subsequent specialized training for interpreting in legal settings.

By the end of the research conversations participants identified significant need for continuing conversation among colleagues, similar to what happened in the focus groups.

5. Next Steps

We will continue to analyse the data, and may conduct further focus groups in order to explore these findings with other groups of experienced interpreters working in legal settings. We will begin to adapt and incorporate the findings into education of interpreters. We believe that training that brings awareness of power and privilege, and explicitly addresses dynamics in interpreted interactions support effective interpreting practice.[3]

References

Bogdan, R. & Biklen, S. (1992). *Qualitative Research for Education: An Introduction to Theory and Methods*, 2nd ed. Boston: Allyn & Bacon.

Brück, P. (2012). Power and responsibility in interpreting situations: The views of Austrian Deaf customers. Paper presented at efsli, September 15, 2012 in Vienna, AU.

De Meulder, M. & Heyerick, I., (2012). Deaf interpreters on television: Challenging power and responsibility. Paper presented at efsli, September 15, 2012 in Vienna, AU.

Coffey, A. & Atkinson, P. (1996). *Making sense of qualitative data: Complementary research strategies*. Thousand Oaks, CA: Sage Publications.

Patton, M. (2002). *Qualitative research and evaluation methods* (3rd ed.). Thousand Oaks, CA: Sage Publications.

Pöchhacker, F. (2004). *Introducing interpreting studies*. London: Routledge.

Savvalidou, F. (2012). Identity issues in sign language interpreting: The power and responsibility of representing the identities of others. Paper presented at efsli, September 15, 2012 in Vienna, AU.

Seleskovitch, D. (1978). *Interpreting for international conferences*. Pen and Booth: Arlington, VA.

Wadensjö, C. (1998). *Interpreting as interaction*. London, England: Longman.

Wilcox, S. & Shaffer, B. (2005). Toward a cognitive model of interpreting. In T. Janzen (Ed.), *Topics in signed language interpreting*, pp. 27-50. Amsterdam, Netherlands: John Benjamins Publishing Co.

---

[3] The researchers wish to thank the study participants – we are grateful for your time, energy and desire to improve interpreting work. Thank you also to research assistants Jennifer Cranston and LeWana Clark, Gallaudet University PhD students, and to Sharon Gervasoni for editing.

Identity Issues in Sign language Interpreting
The Power and Responsibility of Representing the Identities of Others

Flora Savvalidou
Greek Sign Language Interpreter
Greece

Keywords: Identities, Identity Theory Model, Sign Language Interpreters

Abstract

This paper investigates the issues of identities representation in an interpreted situation, using the theoretical framework of the Identity Theory model (Burke & Stets, 2009). Based on a survey that explored the relationship between sign language interpreters' anxiety and their self-talk, it identifies the power and responsibility that this representation entails, and suggests the need of awareness on identity issues for all the professionals involved in the sign language interpreting field, interpreters and their teachers alike. In order to illustrate more vividly the relationship between the interpreters' identity/ies and their power and responsibility, actual quotes from sign language interpreters, as expressed in a research study, will be used.

1. Introduction

Identity Theory was introduced by Burke and Stets (2009); it is a theoretical framework within which identity is conceptualized as a set of meanings attached to the self that serves as a standard or reference that guides behaviour in situations (Stets & Biga, 2003). Based on their model, a research was conducted trying to explore the relationship between self-talk and identity processes in role performance anxiety as experienced by sign language interpreters. This was made possible through the examination of the interpreters' self-talk (the thoughts they have before, during or after their assignments). The research was conducted in 2011 as my final thesis for the EUMASLI program (European Master in Sign Language Interpreting), in which 517 sign language interpreters from Europe, the United States, Canada and Australia participated sharing their thoughts, experiences and insights.

The paper presented here is based on evidence coming from this research and will focus on the aspect of the power, that sign language interpreters hold, their responsibility and the implications that the awareness of this responsibility produces. Additionally it will try to propose the benefits, both professionally and personally, that the application of the Identity Theory model in our field would have.

2. Identity Theory

According to the Identity Theory model people have many identities and these identities are seen as dynamic and constantly negotiated with the environment. Each of our identities is comprised of identity meanings, that is, what it means for us to have this identity. These meanings comprise the identity standard. If we consider the example of the presenter in a conference while she is standing in front of the audience, she could have many identities, the identity of woman, daughter, sister, partner, interpreter, presenter and so on. However, in that specific setting, the one of presenter is the dominant one. Nevertheless, other identities could be also activated, such as wanting to be seen as a beautiful woman. In the case of this presenter, her identity standard meanings could include being clear, interesting, respectable or even impressive. These meanings need to be verified, otherwise the person will try to achieve the verification by modifying her behaviour.

As Burke and Stets claim, every time we interact with the environment one or more identities are activated and a feedback loop is established. The cycle is organized as a control system and people are motivated to bring the meanings of their behaviour into consistency with the meanings of their identities. In other words they try to achieve a semantic congruence between the output to the environment (behaviour) and the inputs they receive as a response (feedback) from the environment. Inputs have the same dimensions of meaning with the ones contained in the identity standard and they are compared with them, with the goal of matching the perception to the standard (Burke & Stets, 2009). Thus, achieving the Identity Verification.

During this process an inner mechanism, the *Comparator*, compares the input perceptions of meanings relevant to the identity with the meanings of the identity standard. It then produces an "error signal," which is the difference between the input and the standard. So, if the standard contains a self-definition in terms of being influential to a given degree, the input function monitors the degree of influence one appears to have in a situation. Since the standard is personal, only the person can tell when her perception matches the standard (Ibid).

In the above example, the person produces an output, i.e. presents her paper at the conference and she receives an input based on how she thinks the others see her performance as a presenter at a conference. Her perceptions include three perspectives: *reflected appraisals* (how we think others see us), *social comparisons* (how we see ourselves in comparison to others), and *self-attributions* (how we see ourselves). After the error signal is produced, that is a discrepancy is detected, for instance she is not as influential a presenter as she would desire according to her successful presenter identity standard, she moderates her behaviour, her output, in order to compensate for that discrepancy. She could, for example, change her style, her tone of voice or her word choices. According to Burke and Stets (ibid), output translates the error into meaningful actions and behaviours that act upon the social situation. The aim of this process is always the Identity Verification.

3. Identity Processes and the Power of Interpreters

Interpreter: A neutral participant or a powerful identities juggler?
As explained above, every time a person interacts with the environment, her identities are activated. In an interaction between persons who speak the same language, when a feedback loop is established, the output, the input and the comparison with the identity standard, are

handled by the person herself. Therefore the person is responsible for her representation and the, possibly, necessary moderation of her behaviour in order to achieve identity verification.

However, in an interpreter-mediated situation/ inter-action, a unique phenomenon is taking place. The two (or more) interactants (i.e. hearing and deaf participants) give away their representation, without even realizing it, to the interpreter. In a sense a double embodiment is taking place where the interpreter is handling the identities of the interactants. As a result the output of the hearing person is represented to the deaf through the interpreter and the input from the deaf (to the feedback loop of the hearing person) is represented to the hearing again mediated through the interpreter. The same happens for the representation of the deaf person to the hearing. In this case the interpreter enacts the identity of the two interlocutors based on her subjective perceptions. In other words, the input to their perspective feedback loops and the consequent data to their comparator are what the interpreter perceived of their language and behaviours and not the participants' output itself as they think. At the same time, the interpreter has to take care of her own feedback loop and make sure that she works towards her own identity verification that is, making sure that her identity standard meanings of interpreter identity are met and she is seen as a very good interpreter.

4. Identity processes in an interpreted situation

Juggling on a tight rope
A survey was conducted in 2011 among sign language interpreters from Europe, USA, Canada and Australia. The survey was in English and employed a mixed methodology using both quantitative and qualitative approaches to understand the relationship between identity processes and anxious self-talk. It consisted of 23 questions that aimed to provide some identity measures, measure the frequency of anxious self-talk and investigate the anxiety-provoking factors in the sign language interpreting profession. The study was open from May until July 2011.

The results are published in the author's master thesis (Savvalidou, 2011).

According to the study two major issues emerged in relation to the identities involved in an interpreted situation. These issues are related to the interpreter's own identities and the responsibility of representing the identity of the deaf person. The second becomes especially anxiety provoking considering the difficulty of a hearing interpreter to fully understand what the deaf identity entails. As Cokely (2008: 71) puts it: "The fact is that that interpreters who are not deaf will never understand what it is like to be deaf."

According to Mason (2005:40), "[...] all participants project an identity via their discourse and other choices [...] all participants perceive the identities of other participants according to their own set of assumptions. Moreover, both these activities are acts of construction and reconstruction." In the case of an interpreted situation between hearing and deaf people, there are at least three identity processes taking place, that of the deaf person, of the hearing person and of the interpreter. The power resulting from this identities' handling exceeds the representation of the participants' identities and can have serious consequences in their lives. As one colleague states:

I need to make sure that I am as accurate as possible. The outcome of this could affect someone's life! What if I make an error that has dire consequences?

4.1 Some issues on Interpreters' identity

In respect to interpreter's identity issues, three aspects can be said to be basic. The first one is the high expectations that the interpreters themselves as well as the people around them have of the interpreters. As Hetherington (2011: 142) puts it "interpreters are expected to perform magic". These expectations affect interpreters' performance, produce anxiety and could make interpreting a real struggle. Some of the statements of the interpreters that participated in the study reveal that their Identity Standard meanings include the interpreter being 'perfect', impressive' or even 'being able to interpret 100%'.

Here follow some direct quotes, in italics, from participants in the survey (see also Savvalidou, 2011) relating to high expectations:

I want to be seen as an experienced interpreter.

I want to do the very best job and impress both deaf client and team.

The consumers are going to be frustrated if I am not perfect.

I may need to interrupt his/her speech in order to get some clarifications. I think something like that raises doubts for the interpreting skills of the interpreter.

I won't be able to translate 100%.

The second issue that is related to the interpreters' identities is that of bringing a second dominant identity to the situation (which influence how he/she is seen as a professional). This other identity could be

- African-American
As an African-American interpreter when I go into certain assignments I do think about my race and what impact, if any, that will have on the assignment. Some consumers may pre-judge my interpreting skills based solely on my race without actually having ever seen me work. Even though I have a B.A. and a M.A. in interpreting they may doubt my abilities to do the work. I often feel like I have more to prove when I walk into an assignment. More to prove and more to lose if I were to do a less than perfect job.

- a friend
In situations where confidentiality is prioritized and I don't know who the Deaf client is I worry it may be a friend and cause some discomfort for all parties involved.

- a woman:
On a perfectly vain front, I'd be worried about how I look.

- a non-Coda interpreter or a Coda interpreter
Will my CODA colleagues see that I do not sign as fluently as they do? They will possibly judge me now.

I have been interpreting, professionally (certified,) for 30+ years. I am sick of all the back stabbing and negativity from hearing interpreters who look down on codas. I am sick of professional trainings, workshops, conferences, etc.
CATERING to the hearing interpreters & completely ignoring professional development needs of coda interpreters. To be honest...I'd rather work alone or with another coda. Working with insecure, threatened hearing interpreters is just too tiring!

- a hearing interpreter working with a deaf interpreter:
When working with a Deaf interpreter who doesn't trust hearing team members or who doesn't process before and after the assignment.
Would they judge me for not taking up their suggestions? Rationale behind that question is that often my Deaf interpreter colleagues are older and have more years of experiences but I disagree with their methods and coping tactics to work as an interpreter. Many of my Deaf interpreting colleagues do not have formal training and rather learned everything "on-the-job" compared to me where I have completed two year interpreting program, so often I dislike knowing that my Deaf interpreting colleagues are in the audience because I do feel they are there to observe me and measure me up.

An important aspect of the activation of other identities during an assignment is that of empathy. Often the interpreter finds herself in a situation where Deaf people are oppressed or treated in an inappropriate manner. In this situation the identity of being a fair person is activated and ethical dilemmas are produced since the interpreter has to remain neutral, as the Code of Ethics states, but at the same time, cannot bear an injustice taking place.

Situations where i don't agree with the content or the opinion mentioned by speakers/signers; situations where oppression and bad power relations are more than obvious.

I feel anxious when I interpret in an environment where I know that the deaf person's or his or her family member's legal rights are being violated.

A third critical issue is that of the "Interpreters' identity crisis" (Hale, 2005). Interpreter identity crisis is caused by ambivalence about the interpreter's role, interpreters' insecurities about their own competence, and a tendency to undermine the interpreting task by the service provider (seeing interpreter as an aid) or the service recipient (interpreter there to help). This crisis can be observed in three basic areas:

- Institutional sphere (setting)
- Professional sphere (code of ethics, professional training, accreditation)
- Interpersonal sphere (participants involved)

According to Hale (Ibid.19) "[...] the most difficult obstacle to overcome in the interpersonal sphere is the self, that natural inclination as a human to reach out and help, to make judgments about who is right and wrong, to ensure fairness, to fix things when they go wrong." As one participant in the survey put it, anxiety is caused in *situations where I don't agree with the content or the opinion mentioned by speakers/signers; situations where oppression and bad power relations are more than obvious.*

4.2 Deaf identity

In order for the interpreter to carry out the representation of the participants' identities she must be very well aware of their culture. In the case of Deaf interactants in an interpreted situation this could be problematic. As Cokely (2008: 71), states:

> "[...] interpreters have become less and less connected with and connected to the Deaf Community. Perhaps our disconnectedness has happened so gradually that we have failed to notice or perhaps this is the inevitable result of the encroachment of an individualistic society in a collectivist Community. Regardless, the consequences remain the same - the less connected we are, the less knowledgeable we are; the less knowledgeable we are, the less effective we are; the less effective we are, the more Deaf people continue to be misunderstood by society at large."

The responsibility the interpreter has in this process of representation is very apparent in the case of the Deaf client as seen in the interpreters' anxious self-talk recorded in the study. The participants' answers show that they are very much aware of the responsibility this representation entails. Interpreters are worried whether the representation is

- appropriate or correct

Not representing the Deaf client in the best light.

Am I representing Deaf/Hearing clients appropriately?

If my hearing clients are thinking the Deaf people are sounding as knowledgeable as they are since I am trying to match them.

I hope I am representing the deaf client's voice correctly.
I am concerned that the Deaf person will get her needs met and that I can represent her correctly.

I hope I do this Deaf client justice when I read them back to voice.

I hope I can do the speakers / signers justice. I hope I can interpret as clearly as they are expressing themselves.

- going to have consequences for the Deaf people
I feel anxious when I interpret in an environment where I know that the deaf person's or his or her family member's legal rights are being violated.

If I make a mistake, the hearing people will think the deaf person isn't as intelligent as they are.

My performance will reflect on the deaf person.

I just don't want any misunderstandings or negative impacts to result from my interpretation.

I hope that I don't make mistakes could have bad consequences for my clients.

My main goal is always to represent my deaf clients well and when I don't perform well, it reflects poorly on them. If the hearing people are not familiar with my client or my role it adds more stress as everything I do will reflect either positively or negatively.

It is noteworthy that this responsibility can result in an unbearable situation for the interpreter as reported in the self-talk of some participants in the study.

I want to escape - help!!

Oh God, I hate this, why did I become an interpreter, I can't stand it, I wish I would disappear down a trap door in the floor, how can I get out of this?

5. Recommendations for application in our field and professional Development

I feel like I am being judged. I feel like they may not be able to separate me as a person from the work that I do.

In the above statement lies the core impact that the development of awareness on identity issues, on the part of interpreters, as well as the application of the Identity Theory model, can have. Interpreters experience a possible failure or a judgment on the professional level as if it were on the level of their personality as a whole. Application of the Identity Theory model and the understanding of issues that sign language interpreters face in terms of identity processes, would contribute in their professional development in multiple areas:

- Consciousness
It would increase understanding of themselves and their awareness of what they want to take for themselves from the situation.

- Awareness
Interpreters could develop a better awareness of the identity issues that each participant brings into the situation.

- Training and life-long practice
As Hale (2005) states "training teaches the lay person to do what does not come normal". In that sense training of sign language interpreters could benefit from Identity Theory model as it would help interpreters understand better the interpreted situation as well as the participants of the interaction and especially themselves into it. More specifically this knowledge could help interpreters to:

- Work on themselves (mainly on the size of their identification). Interpreters could be trained to realize that whatever happens in the situation has to do with their professional identity and not who they are as persons.

- Know what to ask their clients. When they realize the essential part that the negotiation of identities play in an interaction they can be more clear on what information to ask for in order to represent more accurately the participants' identities.
- Reduce the part of themselves that they bring into the situation. When they understand that more than one identity is activated in each situation, they can become more able to reduce their interference by recognizing which identities are activated and which are not related to the interpretation itself.

- Work with the ethical dilemmas on a different basis. When examined under the light of Identity Theory, the ethical dilemmas could be seen as totally different issues. It could even turn out that we cannot speak of ethical dilemmas at all. For example, if an interpreter finds herself in a frustrating situation where she has to be neutral as the Code of Ethics says but, at the same time, has to watch the oppressing behaviour of the hearing person and not being able to intervene. Examining such a case in terms of identities, the interpreter could separate the interpreter identity where the standard is that she has to remain neutral, from the 'being a fair person' identity according to which you cannot watch an injustice taking place without doing anything to help. This separation may not provide the right reaction per se, but provides a tool to use, choosing to verify the identity that ranks higher. Thus it could help the interpreter take a decision that can later be justified to herself and others, and develop her meta-awareness on her decision-making. On a second level, she can later decide if this decision was right, given the circumstances, and develop a criterion for future decisions. As a result the dilemma is not a decision between two rights but between two identities activated and which of the two ranks higher in the personal value system of the interpreter.

- Revisit identity meanings (machine, bicultural, ally[4]). The different interpreter models could be examined under a new framework that is, by defining the identity standard meanings each of them contains. This way the interpreter but also the interpreters' community as a whole could decide which model is the appropriate one for a situation in order for the hearing and deaf identities to be effectively represented and negotiated in this situation.

- Be familiar with the issues that will arise. When the situations are not examined as a separate case each time, but as a combination of the identities involved in them, the interpreters have a tool to understand them and compare, evaluate, decide upon, and consequently act upon them. Thus, their decisions are not based on a subjective situation-specific understanding but on a model with which they can communicate with the other colleagues and develop a general view on the interpreting situations.

- Stress management. Interpreting is one of the more stressful professions for many reasons, some of which have been already mentioned above. One of the main reasons is the responsibility interpreters have of being a catalyst in any interpreted situation. The survey study showed that anxiety is directly connected with identity issues. Understanding the identity dynamics involved in a situation could help interpreters deal more effectively with these issues and address the root of them instead of blaming themselves for not being up to the standards.

Finally, interpreters who have managed to understand their

---

[4] For further reading on the relation between power and interpreter's models (or in the frame of Identity Theory, identity meanings) see Baker-Shenk (1991) 'The interpreter: Machine, advocate, or ally?' Also see Napier (2006), 'Sign Language Interpreting: Linguistic Coping Strategies.'

identities and how they are manifested, and who are able to make the distinction between their professional and personal identities, can be more aware of their power, more relaxed with their responsibility, can increase their decision latitude, feel more confident with their choices, handle their stress more effectively, communicate their needs more clearly, address them more successfully and as a result: live a happier life.

References

Baker-Shenk, C. (1991). The Interpreter: Machine, advocate, or ally. In Jean
Plant-Moeller (Ed), *Expanding Horizons: Proceedings of the 1991 RID Convention* (pp. 120-140). Silver Spring, MD: RID Publications.
Burke, P. and Stets, J. (2009). *Identity Theory*. New York: Oxford University Press.
Cokely, D. (2008). Never Our Language, Never Our Culture: The Importance of Deaf Community Connectedness for Interpreters. In C. J. Kellett Bidoli & E. Ochse (Eds.), *English in International Deaf Communication*, pp. 57-73. Bern: Peter Lang.
Hale, S. (2005). The Interpreter's Identity Crisis. In J. House, M. R. M. Ruano & N. Baumgarten (Eds.), *Translation and the Construction of Identity*, pp. 14-29. IATIS. Korea.
Hetherington, A. (2011). A Magical Profession? Causes and Management of Occupational Stress in the Signed Language Interpreting Profession. In L. Leeson, S. Wurm & M. Vermeerbergen (Eds.), *Signed Language Interpreting Preparation, Practice and Performance,* pp. 138-159. Manchester: St. Jerome Publishing.
Mason, I. (2005). Projected and Perceived Identities in Dialogue Interpreting'. In J. House, M. R. M. Ruano & N. Baumgarten (Eds.), *Translation and the Construction of Identity Translation and the Construction of Identity*, pp. 30-52. IATIS. Korea
Napier, J. (2002). *Sign Language Interpreting: Linguistic Coping Strategies.*
Gloucestershire: Douglas McLean.
Savvalidou, F. (2011). *Relationship Between Self-Talk and Identity*

Processes in Role Performance Anxiety As Experienced By Sign Language Interpreters. Unpublished Master's thesis. EUMASLI. Magdeburg-Stendal University.

Stets, J. & Biga, C.F. (2003). Bringing Identity Theory into Environmental Sociology. *Sociological Theory,* 21, 398-423.

Issues of power and responsibilities in sign language interpreting within sign language users' communities

Patricia Shores Hermann
HfH – University of Applied Sciences of
Special Needs Education
Zürich, Switzerland

Keywords: Power, responsibility, professional interpreting

Abstract
The aim of this paper is to contribute to a better understanding of how the issues of power and responsibilities in sign language interpreting emerge, as well as to address the questions of why and when interpreters use power in their professional setting. Moreover, there is a necessity in updating the use of the term for 'power` in signed languages to match the current Best Practices within the sign language interpreting field.
The term 'power' is used here both as a measure of influence and of control over outcomes, resources and capabilities. Moreover the term 'responsibility' adds to the discussion of professional behaviours in using these powers. These powers and responsibilities are first looked at theoretically. The following discussion is guided by ten thinking processes (or mind sets), which play a significant role in establishing power status within sign language user communities.

1. Introduction: Concepts involved in the terms 'power' and 'responsibility'

The concepts of 'power' and 'responsibility' need to be looked at in terms of their meanings for the professional interactions between interpreters and clients/consumers. Hofstede's book *Power Distance* (1993) talks of power as being "a measure of influence or control over outcomes as well as control over resources and capabilities." The Cambridge on-line dictionary's definition of responsibility is "...the professional behaviours dealing with the responsibility, including the position of authority over someone and/or having a duty to make certain that particular things are done".

Huntington (2002), in discussing the issues of power in Western societies, emphasises that human beings need security and stability. The power of one person or a group over someone or something can mean their behaviour will change the situation as a result of persuasion, encouragement and/or force. Power can enable control over several significant resources including social and cultural activities. Cultures deal with and behave differently toward the concept of power. The law of supply and demand affects power distribution. Power is also involved in the movements of people.

Pfeffer (2010) offers many helpful insights into the theory of power. He cites the social psychologist McClelland (1976) who considers power to be a fundamental human drive, which – while varying across individuals – is found in people from many different cultures alongside of a need for achievement. Pfeffer explains that "Will - the drive to take on big challenges, and skill, the capabilities required to turn ambition into accomplishment .The three personal qualities embodied in will are ambition, energy and focus" (Ibid, p.43). Five additional skills are also used in acquiring power: "Self-knowledge; reflective mind set; confidence and the ability to project self-assurance; ability to read others and empathize with their point of view and capacity to tolerate conflict" (Ibid: 43).

2. The question of power and interpreting

The communication between the deaf/sign language users and hearing customers relies on the interpreter/s. Hoffmeister (2008) states that "the interpreting process conveyed with great power and sometimes great confusion" (p.204). He emphasizes that "The interpreter is in almost absolute control of the communication process. The interpreter controls [...] who speaks when, what languages will be used and what will be actually be 'said' between the Deaf and the hearing participants" (Ibid: 204).

The discrepancy of knowledge of the participants involved in these settings brings up questions of whether the interpreters are being neutral in issues of power or control. Roy (1989, 1993) stated: "The interpreters function as participants within the discourse, regulating turns". Wadensjö (1992) reinforced this by her findings that "interpreters alter contributions in ways that are designed to meet interactional goals established by the participants."

Is there a legitimate justification for sign language interpreters to assume this power status professionally and, if so, how can they use this status properly, effectively and fairly without lessening the power of sign language users?

The following ten groups of thinking processes or 'mind sets' (Shores, 1992) are a first attempt to look at the power status of sign language interpreters and of the communities of sign language users. The examples for these mind sets are drawn from socio-economic, political and cultural facets of European societies and clearly show the interrelationship between the power of interpreters and the increasing empowerment of stakeholders (the deaf or sign language users and/or hearing consumers of the interpreting services). The selected literature references are also included.

3. Ten 'Mind sets'

The Cambridge on-line dictionary's definition of 'mind set' is *"a person's way of thinking and their opinions"*. It reflects an individual's or a society's mental attitude or a habit deciding how he/she will interpret and respond to a situation. The ten mind sets discussed below are presented in the form of alternatives, pairing more traditional ways with more modern ways of looking at the sign language user and the interpreter.

3.1 Mind set: medical to social view of deafness

The first mind set involves two different societal views of the signing community - the traditional medical and the more recent social model (Lane 1992). A society's attitude towards disabled/Deaf people shapes the relationship between Deaf people and the sign language interpreter in these different models. Kushalnagar and Rashid (2008) portray the differing status of deaf persons in two different kinds of interactions (p.43). The first interaction is of the deaf person in a 'powerless' capacity like a child in school, a patient in hospital or a client receiving mental health services. The second interaction is intended to help interpreters who want to avoid this kind of stereotyping behaviour by becoming aware of the attitudes and beliefs that encourage the paternalistic behaviour characteristic of the medical model and by undertaking conscious efforts to counter the stereotypes that apply to both the interpreters and the Deaf consumers.

3.2 Mind set: homogenised community to cultural plurality

The second mind set is related to the fact that, as a result of migration and globalisation, sign language (SL) communities are changing from being homogenised communities to reflecting cultural plurality.

This change involves the use of language for new purposes and brings new challenges to SL communities. Evolving multimedia and internet technologies are also enabling the signer to share a wide variety of different and distinctive local, regional, national and international signs, and are giving the concept of 'Deaf community' a new international meaning (Valentine & Skelton, 2008).

3.3 Mind set: patronization to partnership

The third mind set reflects a change from patronization to partnership as Deaf people/sign language users adopt more active and independent life styles. These new life styles create a corresponding need for modern interpreting services that empower the users, increasingly giving them control of communication events, which, in turn, continues to further the shift from patronization to partnership. As Napier, Carmichael and Wiltshire (2008:23) put it, the interpreter empowers the consumer with information.

3.4 Mind set: barriers to accessibility

The fourth mind set concerns a move from barriers to accessibility. This mind set reflects the expectations that interpreters are requested to fulfil in form of communication access in formal settings such as universities, hospitals or law courts. Here, there is still a discrepancy in power status. As Napier et al. put it (2008: 22):

> "The deaf person is not in a position of power or authority in these discussions [...] he/she is either a student or patient, defendant or witness [...] he/she is not the expert in those settings [...], he/she is relying on the expertise of others during those specific setting namely educational interpreting (cf. Winston, 2004), medical setting (cf. Metzger, 1999), legal setting (cf. Russell, 2002) and community interpreting (cf. Harrington & Turner, 2001)."

3.5 Mind set: dependence to independence

The fifth mind set deals with moving from dependence to independence, which requires the change of roles and power distribution. Kushalnager and Rashi (2008) remind us that many interpreters are used to work with deaf individuals who are in the client role. The deaf professionals (emancipated from the client role) perform the dynamic changes in roles of leading the communication. Somehow for some, "...this new distribution of power often brings discomfort to the interpreter..." (p.50). Corker (2000) writes that traditionally interpreters have had an advantage over deaf persons due to their role as being the experts and coordinators of the interaction between deaf and hearing people (Kushalnager, et al. 2008:50). As the client becomes more independent, this advantage diminishes. Hauser & Hauser (2008) recommend that both the interpreter and the deaf professional: "[...] have to discover and maintain the fine line with a healthy balance [...] to maximize both partners' abilities to work effectively [...] (p.12). While, as McIntire and Sanderson (1993) point out, in this situation it is the interpreter's role to empower deaf individuals, Deaf individuals must also empower interpreters by taking joint responsibility, showing commitment and tolerance in order to achieve a successful relationship (as cited in Hauser et al. 2008:12).

3.6 Mind set: monolingualism to multilingualism

The sixth mind set concerns the shift from monolingualism to multilingualism. Huntington (2002) states that it is essential to know more than one language in these times of globalisation. One contributor to the blog *Lifofaterp* (Life as an interpreter) summed it up with the phrase "Language is Power". Interpreters of any languages must be aware that language both is power and, in turn, has power. It grants the power to access vast quantities of knowledge and education. The interpreter must also mediate between the power of two languages, by being aware of biases or prejudices in favour of or against either of the languages. It includes the cultural aspects as well.

3.7 Mind set: isolation to alliances

The seventh mind set looks at the move from isolation to alliances. Many societal factors contribute to imbalances and discrimination, which contribute to unfair outcomes in certain interpreting situations. Mindess (1999:170-171) notes the following, "Even though the imbalance of power between our Deaf and hearing consumers is not in within our control, there is a power relationship in which we are intimately involved and over which we may exercise some control". A recent partnership agreement as of 22nd May 2010 between EUD and EFSLI does offer some hope in the efforts to correct existing societal imbalances specifically regarding sign language interpreting.

3.8 Mind set: fragmented to centralised resources

The eighth mind set concerns the change from fragmented to centralised resources. For the field, this move toward more centralised resources represents a new paradigm in thinking and responding to supply and demand. Hurwitz (2008) wrote of the new expectation that Deaf individuals as the consumers of interpreter services must provide input and participate in the decision-making matters related to the interpreting services. It also includes the planning and evaluation of the interpreting services.

3.9 Mind set: cannot to can

The ninth mind set, cannot to can, is an on-going challenge for the users.

Witter-Merithew writes in her weblog that Deaf people/sign language users need "to proceed with higher self-confidence and self-trust and build upon the philosophy that it is possible to perform whatever one wishes". The consequences for interpreters would *be* that they engage in more due diligence – i.e. give a greater level of attention and care to the competent professional exercise to avoid harm to the consumers of their service. According to Witter-Merithew, this would entail recognising that there may be a need for an intervention, taking responsibility, planning a course of action and then taking action.

3.10 Mind set: minimal to maximal standards

The tenth mind set is the change from minimal standards to maximal standards. Interpreters are expected to do their best in each interpreting performance, but this needs to be a two way process. Sign language communities should see an ongoing development stressing the cultivation of their use of sign languages and an enrichment of their sign language cultures.

4. European Preliminary Survey

A European-wide EUD preliminary survey (May/June 2012) led by Hermann-Shores and Fielding-Jackson was aimed at European deaf leaders and focused on the issues of power and responsibilities. This EUD survey written report[1] provided data on their current thinking of European sign language interpreters and the types of power they use. It provided information on the degree to which those respondents perceived whether and how interpreters are consciously aware of their use of power. It also looked at the different phases of the interpreting process (preparatory, performance and completion/reflection) during which this consciousness occurred.

A selection of those significant findings from this survey follow below:
- There is evidence to suggest that there is a tendency to be dependent on interpreters' services, an issue which needs to be tackled in a careful manner. European Deaf leaders see the need for shifting power from interpreters to Deaf consumers.
- Respondents expect sign language interpreters to follow and perform according to the expected ethics of the field. They trust the standard of ethics and performance provided by professional interpreters. However, expectations and trust rest upon the ability of the training institutions and practices to ensure the proper implementation of this code of ethics, professional attitudes, issues of power and responsibilities.
- Deaf consumers need on-going training on how to use sign language interpreting services effectively. An issue for EUD consideration is a European-wide training project focused on the theme of empowering deaf consumers in using interpreting services properly.
- Interpreters are expected to be trained in authentic and

---

[1] Hermann-Shores and Jackson-Fielding submitted the final preliminary survey report with detailed findings to Mark Wheatley, EUD Executive Director on Monday 10th December 2012. The follow up will be arranged with the new EUD Board during the summer of 2013.

realistic cultural settings (i.e. within deaf organisations, meetings and programs). It is not enough if they graduate from universities or higher degree programs without real and sufficient contact with deaf users.

5. Final thoughts

Going back to the question posed at the beginning of this article: Is there a legitimate justification for sign language interpreters to convey this power status professionally? How can they use this status properly, effectively and fairly without disempowering Deaf consumers? The summary of the preliminary survey indicates that interpreters are not neutral. Hence, it seems that the issues of power and responsibilities depend upon implementing the Code of Ethics properly. Findings from past research by authors within the sign language interpreter and the sign language user communities should be made more available to all consumers of the services. Sign language communities have the responsibility to empower themselves and to contribute to the ongoing development of sign language interpreting services.

My recommendation is to set up a permanent, professional training as lifelong learning for consumers. This should be a partnership with EUD-EFSLI and would be a consumer educational training project focusing on how to maximise the benefits of using interpreters and interpreting services. It should promote the understanding of how interpreting processes take place, so that consumers can maximise their communicative goals to achieve their purpose of communication. It empowers Deaf/sign language consumers so those both deaf and hearing consumers know and apply their rights. It provides on-going professional training for interpreters. This aim for such a cooperative project is a WIN-WIN situation, ensuring that the different power bases are utilised properly, fairly and effectively. Otherwise we will face the continuation of imbalanced uses of powers and responsibilities for all parties involved.

References

Cambridge on-line Dictionary,
   http://dictionary.cambridge.org/dictionary/british/power_1?q=power.
   Retrieved May 2012.
   http://dictionary.cambridge.org/dictionary/british/mindset?q=mindset.
   Retrieved June 2013.
Corker, M. (2000). Disability politics, language planning, and inclusive social policy. *Disability and Society, 15* (3), 445-462.
EUD/EFLSI Partnership Agreement,
   http://www.efsli.org/efsli/partners/partners.php. Retrieved June 2013
Hauser, A. B. & Hauser, P. C. (2008). The Deaf Professional-Designated Interpreter Model. In P. C. Hauser (Ed.), *Deaf Professionals and Designated Interpreters – a new paradigm* (pp. 3-21). Washington, D. C.: Gallaudet University Press.
Hermann-Shores, P. & Fielding-Jackson, E. (2012). *Survey Report to EUD: Power and Responsibilities in the field of Sign language Interpreting.* (Unpublished report).
Hoffmeister, R. (2008). Border Crossing by Hearing Children of Deaf Parents. The Lost History of Codas. In H.-D. L. Baumann (Ed.), *Open Your Eyes. Deaf Studies Talking* (pp. 189-215). Minneapolis: University of Minnesota Press.
Hofstede, G. (1993). *Interkulturelle Zusammenarbeit. Kulturen, Organisationen, Management.* Wiesbaden: Gabler.
Huntington, S. P. (2002). *Kampf der Kulturen. Die Neugestaltung der Weltpolitik im 21. Jahrhundert.* München: Goldmann.
Hurwitz, T. A. (2008). Foreword. In P. C. Hauser (Ed.), *Deaf Professionals and Designated Interpreters – a new paradigm* (pp. vii-x). Washington, D. C.: Gallaudet University Press.
Kushalnagar, P. & Rashid, K. (2008). Attitudes and Behaviors of Deaf Professionals and Interpreters. In P. C. Hauser (Ed.), *Deaf Professionals and Designated Interpreters – a new paradigm* (pp. 43-57). Washington, D. C.: Gallaudet University Press.
Lane, H. (1992). *The Mask of Benevolence. Disabling the Deaf Community.* New York: Vintage.

Lifofaterp Blog, *Language is Power*. Retrieved May 2012 http://www.tumblr.com/tagged/sign-language-interpreter/

McIntire, M. & Sanderson, G. (1993). Bye-bye Bi-bi! Questions of Empowerment and Role. In Registry of Interpreters for the Deaf (RID) (Ed.), *Proceedings of the 1993 RID Convention* (pp. 94-118). Alexandria: RID Publications.

Metzger, M. (1999). *Sign Language Interpreting. Deconstructing the Myth of Neutrality.* Washington, D. C.: Gallaudet University Press.

Mindess, A. (1999). *Reading Between the Signs. Intercultural Communication for Sign Language Interpreters.* Yarmouth: Intercultural Press.

Napier, J., Carmichael, A. & Wiltshire, A. (2008). Look – Pause – Nod. A Linguistic Case Study of a Deaf Professional and Interpreters Working Together. In P. C. Hauser (Ed.), *Deaf Professionals and Designated Interpreters – a new paradigm* (pp. 22-42). Washington, D. C.: Gallaudet University Press.

Pfeffer, J. (2010). *Power. Why some people have it and others don't.* New York: Harper Business.

Roy, C. (1989). *A sociolinguistic analysis of the interpreter's role in the turn exchanges of an interpreted event.* Washington, D. C.: Georgetown University.

Roy, C. (1993). A sociolinguistic analysis of the interpreter's role in simultaneous talk in interpreted interaction. *Multilingual Matters, 12* (4), 341-363.

Shores, P. (1992). Das Jahrzehnt der grossen Schritte. Unmögliches wird möglich? Speech given at the Generalversammlung des Zürcher Fürsorgevereins für Gehörlose. *Gehörlosen-Zeitung, (*15/16), pp.1-2.

Turner, G. H. (2007). Professionalization of interpreting with the community. Refining the model. In C. Wadensjö (Ed.), *The Critical Link 4. Selected Papers from the 4th International Conference on Interpreting in Legal, Health and Social Service Settings, Stockholm, Sweden, 20-23 May 2004* (pp. 181-192). London: Benjamin.

Valentine, G. & Skelton, T. (2008). Changing Spaces. The role of the internet in shaping Deaf geographies. *Social & Cultural Geography, 9* (5), 469-485.

Wadensjö, C. (1992). *Interpreting as interaction. On dialogue-interpreting in immigration hearings and medical encounters*. Linköping: Linköping University.

Witter-Merithew's Weblog, Retrieved February 2012 http://www.streetleverage.com/2012/02/sign-language-interpreters-are-acts-of-omission-a-failure-of-duty

The Power of the Profession, taken for granted?

Ingeborg Skaten
Bergen University College, Norway

Keywords: Power, profession, jurisdiction, trust, Sign Language Interpreters' role

Abstract

In this article, based on my presentation at the efsli conference 2012, some core aspects regarding the Sign Language (SL) Interpreters role and profession are discussed, like: what constitutes a profession and what kind of power does a profession hold?
A profession's power to define the work, manifested in the code of professional conduct, is part of its jurisdiction. Now, in Norway, the main employer of SL-interpreters (NAV) has signalled the need for a new code of ethics for the interpreters and thereby challenging the profession's jurisdiction.
Furthermore, it serves as a classic example of how external sources try to influence or rather change the profession. According to social research, different discourses will always struggle to define and redefine a profession. By highlighting these processes, my project is to provoke a debate on who is to define the interpreter's role and profession. If we, the interpreters, don't, others will.

1. Introduction

This article is based on my presentation at the efsli-conference 2012, where 'Power and Responsibility in the field of Sign Language Interpreting' was the topic. Looking back, it strikes me that responsibility tends to be emphasized in the discourse that define the interpreters role, in so many ways, first and foremost in the way we carry out our profession and not the least in the relationship to the Deaf community. Power, however, is a concept dealt with not without a certain ambiguity, it seems. That is, when interpreters talk about power, it often is in terms of something we should 'be aware of' – which gives me the impression that 'power' is understood as the interpreter's ability to take control in the situation, in a way that is undermining the empowerment of the Deaf client[1].

This is not the perspective on power I discuss in this presentation, as a starting point for debate. On the contrary – my focus is not on the individual interpreter and her/his professional conduct, but rather on the profession and the power it holds. What kind of 'power' might that be? What does it take to claim such power? I will state that we need to address the questions raised here. And given the fact that a profession has to be defined and redefined, according to the sociology of professions, the crucial question for us to debate, will be: Who is defining the Profession of Sign Language interpreters?

2. Our common heritage

It all started in the Deaf society, our history as Sign Language (SL) interpreters share a common heritage. Before interpreting became an occupation, or paid work at least, it was all about volunteering, which left Deaf people in a debt of gratitude. Not a very healthy relationship, for either part, I would say.

In our welfare state to day, Norwegian legislation ensures that Deaf people have the right to interpreter services, and interpreting has become a professional occupation – which also empowers the Deaf, taking part in the majority/hearing society on more even terms. But none of this would have been the case had it not been for the Deaf association that initiated both the interpreter training and the public interpreter service for the Deaf.

And, as history shows, the first SL interpreters came from the Deaf

---

[1] When using the term 'client', I refer to both the hearing and deaf participants in the communication situation that the interpreter relates to. In Norway we say *tolkebruker*, which could be translated into 'user' of the interpreter's service.

"garden" - the apple did not fall far from the tree. Today they are mainly imported from the majority society. For some years now, students can enrol for the BA program in Sign Language and interpreting without any experience in the field, just motivated to learn the language and wanting to become an interpreter. This is far from the situation when the first training courses drew people, all of them familiar with Sign Language and the Deaf community in advance. And for many years, the Deaf association and the interpreters worked closely together in the early days of the profession to be. However, somewhere along the road the interpreters had to break out – to form their own association, constructing their professional identity.

Alongside this development, during the last 30 years or so, the Norwegian Deaf have been fighting for recognition of their language and culture – a struggle parallel with the interpreters' professionalization. Analysing these processes, I find that the professionalization of the interpreters – resulting in higher status for the group, also enhanced the Deaf organizations political work for getting Sign Language officially recognized – and vice versa.

3. Interlocking discourses

I will argue that the discourses that define respectively the Deaf and the interpreters, were - and still are – interlocking. By that I mean: the way we define the interpreter, also in a way define the Deaf. Take the title, 'Sign Language interpreter'. We, the interpreters *for the deaf*, as we used to call ourselves, adopted the new title from our colleagues in Sweden at the time the Deaf Power movement reached the Norwegian Deaf society and the awareness of Sign Language rose amongst Deaf people. A coincidence? Hardly.

The new title emphasized that we, like any other interpreters – say French or Arabic-interpreters, were working with *languages*. As well as recognition of Sign Language, the new title also marks a shift towards regarding both Deaf and hearing as clients and equal parts in the communication situation we were to interpret. Some might say it is entirely indifferent what title we choose, it is what we *do* that matters. That may be, but as a wise man once said: "We do things with words, and words do things to us". Words also manifest in structures, which regulate the field in question. Even a profession has its outset in words. Andrew Abbott (1988:81) puts it like this: "To say a Profession exists, is to make it one".

3.1 Did you say 'profession'?

What the researcher meant by this was to state that a profession is a social construction. It is not God given and neither regulated by the laws of nature. It is constructed by people, in a given society and at a certain time in history. According to Abbott (1988:7), a basic way of explaining what constitutes a profession would be: an occupational group with some special skill. Most scholars will agree on that and underline the correlation between the length of the training required and the status of the profession. One classic example would be the doctor's higher status than the nurse, given their education. Of course, it also has something to do with the *gender* dominating the profession as well.

Another researcher on professions, Harold Wilensky (1964), claims that an occupational group has to go through certain *stages* to become a profession:
- Full time occupation
- Formal training, provided within universities
- Local and then national associations are formed as the core tasks are defined in competition with neighbouring occupations
- Political activity leads to legally controlled licensing and certification
- Formal code of ethical practicing developed

Wilensky did not offer any arguments for why the stages listed above had to be in this order and for that he has been criticised. I find these stages useful as a checklist when discussing whether an occupation may be said to be a profession or not, regardless the order of the stages.

Now – let us move on to our next core concept, namely 'power' and investigate what kind of power a profession holds or rather what it is that constitute a profession's power?

3.2 Power, what 'power'?

According to the sociology of professions, there are three main factors to consider: expertise, jurisdiction and trust. *Expertise* is a corner stone in the professional body. The occupational group has to have special skills and knowledge, acquired from studies in the higher educational system, as we have seen.

Jurisdiction – what is that all about? It is about the profession's right to define the work, to decide who is to be a member on which criteria, and to draw boundaries to other occupational groups/professions. An example: The Norwegian parliament once discussed a proposal on how to improve Deaf people's access to SL interpreters. There it was suggested that family members as interpreters could be the solution. This proposal awoke protest, both from the interpreter association and the Deaf organization. The Deaf spokesperson underlined that interpreting is now a profession; the interpreter has to be educated and competent (Skaten, 2005). Why did the Deaf organization argue like this? Rather than taking care of the interpreters' interest, I see this as a statement declaring that Deaf people are through with being dependent on volunteers.

So - this can also be seen as an example of the mutual interest of the interpreters and the Deaf in defending the profession, drawing boundaries – claiming jurisdiction. By doing so, the Deaf organization demonstrated trust in the profession as well. And *trust* – given from the society (here: both the Deaf- and hearing society), is what legitimates the power of the profession. Without trust, the profession has no power to put behind its claims for jurisdiction. Before the professionalization of the interpreters, Deaf people trusted the *person* they asked to interpret, because they knew him or her. Today, both Deaf and hearing clients basically have to trust the *profession*. In order to do so, they have to know what the profession stands for; what they can expect from an interpreter, what does an interpreter actually do - and what is the interpreter not to do?

This is, as we know, what is expressed in the professions *code of ethic*, or rules of professional conduct. By publishing these, the profession also exercise the power of defining the work.

3.3 Sources of change

Wilensky (1964) argues that there cannot be a profession without a national association. This is the prerequisite of public or legal claims, is also stressed by Abbott (1988). However, having established an association, the social structure of the profession is not fixed. It is constantly under various pressures of marked demands, specialization and inter-professional competition. Abbott (ibid) finds that change within organizations occurs through two sources: external factors: initiating the "opening or closing (of) areas for jurisdiction", and by existing or new professions "seeking new ground" (ibid: 90). Here we shall focus on *external factors* and as an example I will introduce you to a relevant situation in Norway these days, which calls for debate. But first, let me give you a brief presentation of the Norwegian model of organizing the public interpreter service.

4. The Norwegian model

NAV, the Norwegian labour and welfare administration, is given the responsibility for rendering interpreter services for the Deaf, deaf and blind, and deafened people as a 'compensatory aid' for their loss of hearing/their handicap.

Much could be said about the handicap discourse versus the language/minority discourse, defining the Deaf – but let us leave that for now and concentrate on NAV's role. In spite of the fact that Norway may have one of the best public interpreter-services, there is still a lack of interpreters to meet the demand from the clients. Therefore, the interpreter-service has to act as *gatekeepers*, deciding who is to have an interpreter and who is not.

So – NAV holds a great deal of power when it comes to allocating interpreters, on the one hand, and on the other: as an employer of SL interpreters. Most positions for SL-interpreters you will find within the NAV-system at the interpreter-service with bureaus all over the country. Also, the freelancers have to have a contract with NAV to get paid. This means that practically all of the practising SL interpreters in Norway are related to NAV, directly or indirectly. This somewhat special market situation might result in blurring the boundaries of the profession versus the employing institution – in that case: what about the power of the profession?

4.1 Challenging the jurisdiction

We have seen that one of the core features of the power of a profession is to define the work and to draw boundaries to other professions. And we have also seen that a profession always will be under pressure from external sources, wanting to challenge its jurisdiction.

This, I will argue, is exactly what is going on in Norway these days. In 2011 NAV issued a report (unpublished) as a first step to restructure and improve the access to interpreters for the Deaf. The report outlines several constructive suggestions on improving the interpreter-service. When this part was presented for the Deaf association, these suggestions were most welcomed.

However, a certain part of the report regarding the interpreter's *role,* have not been given much attention. At least not until the Norwegian deaf magazine published an article where I questioned the implications of some suggestions in the report, hoping to provoke a debate on the subject (Døves Tidsskrift, 1/2012). You can read about this in Elisabet Tiselius' blog, in English[2]. In the report NAV is advocating for the need of a *new code of ethic* for their interpreters, and they also suggest that the training programs, the interpreter education, should "broaden the interpreters perspective on the interpreter's role, and their competencies" (my translation). This is interesting. Here is NAV initiating an opening of the professions area of jurisdiction, wanting to redefine the interpreter's role. In short, as I read it, it is about giving the interpreter responsibility for evaluating the communication situation and they should report any problems, so that the Deaf can be helped coping better.

I find this a bit disturbing, to say the least, both the implications of the suggestions – regarding the clients trust in the interpreters neutrality and confidentiality and the fact that these suggestions have not been subject for an open discussion in the interpreters association, until recently. Why is that so? One should think that the organization representing the SL interpreters' professional interests, would engage in discussions regarding the interpreters' role. When they did not, one explanation could have to do with blurring of the professions boundaries, given the marked situation. Anyway, I am happy to say it is on the board's agenda now and a discussion is coming up.

4.2 Defining – and redefining the profession

I see what is happening in Norway as just one example of how external factors exert pressure on the professions jurisdiction. You may have other examples from your countries on how the market, or competing professions, tries to influence the interpreter's role.

My agenda is to draw attention to structures that have impact on our profession, and that we should be aware of. And, we should bear in mind that the public *trust* in us, is what legitimates the profession. The

---

[2] Elisabet Tiselius is a conference interpreter, PhD student and lecturer at Bergen University.

professions code of ethic is the contract between the SL interpreters and the clients. Now NAV signals a need for a new set of code of ethic. Where will that leave the interpreter? In between the profession's and the employer's demands, I guess. More important, even: Sign Language interpreters today have come a long way from being regarded as the Deaf 'helpers'. Now we may be witnessing a shift in paradigm given NAV's intention to "broaden" the perspective on the interpreter's role, assigning them responsibility beyond interpreting. Where will that leave us – and the Deaf client?

I am *not* saying that the profession should not change, or that the interpreter's role is fixed, of course not. And, naturally the profession must meet the given society's demand, at any time. As Abbott states; a profession has to be defined and redefined, over and over again. The question is: Who should have the power to do so?

5. Conclusion

There were 14 different countries represented in the workshop in the parallel session where I held my presentation. They worked together in groups, discussing some questions relating to my theme. Let me give you a brief summary.

The groups were to debate on whether SL interpreters in their respective country could be said to form a profession or not. Not surprisingly, their answers show that there are great differences within Europe, let alone the world. In some countries, SL interpreters form a profession in every respect, in others, I would say it is in the making.

Anyway, it seems that SL interpreters experience pressure from external factors wanting to define their work, regardless differences in the way they are organized (or not). So, we may conclude that the question about the professions' power, are not merely of academic interest. The discussion shows that there is absolutely no reason to take the power of the profession for granted!

References

Abbott, A. (1988). *The System of Professions: An Essay on the Division of Expert Labour*. Chicago: The University of Chicago Press.
NAV, www.nav.no
Skaten, I. (2012). NAV vil utvide tolkerollen, med hvilke konsekvenser? *Døves Tidsskrift 1/2012, 16-17*.
Skaten, I. (2005). *Tolk, døvetolk eller tegnspråktolk?: En diskurs-analytisk undersøkelse av identitetskonstruksjon hos tolkestudenter*. Hovedfagsoppgave, Sosiologisk institutt, Universitetet i Bergen.
Tiselius, Elisabet *Redefinition of the (Sign Language) interpreter's role?* Retrieved June 1, 2012. Blogg: http://interpretings.net/
Wilensky, H. (1964). The professionalization of everyone? *American Journal of Sociology*, 70, 137-138.

Abstracts

Deaf-Hearing Interpreter Teams: Celebrating Our Ties

Christopher Tester & Sharon Neumann Solow
Contact: Tester.Christopher@gmail.com

Deaf and hearing interpreter (DI-HI) teams provide a critical service that is revolutionizing the field of interpreting. As we learn and grow as a profession, we must continue to offer opportunities for open discussion and learning to become more sophisticated regarding this crucial area of work.

This workshop will explore the principles and skills involved in working as a DI-HI team. We will discuss approaches for individual, team, small group and organizational development. Participants will have an opportunity to air thoughts, suggestions and any concerns they may have. The trainers will offer stimulus materials for discussion and for applied practice of theoretical learning.

This presentation will go through some of the basic challenges and benefits of Deaf-Hearing teaming. Our discussion will cover some basic Do's and Don'ts and discussion of ethical and role challenges that may confront DI-HI teams.

We will focus on teamwork and collaborative, cooperative approaches to the work we do. Within this frame we will focus on skills, knowledge and attitudes that are necessary for effective teaming and, more importantly, successful interpretation in general. We will explore the concepts of collaboration, complementation and compensation as it relates to HI-DI teams as well as challenges in language processing and prosody. The challenges regarding chunking, memory, eye-contact and natural prosody are unique for Deaf-Hearing teams. We will discuss and, if time permits, practice some teaming tasks, focusing on these areas of concern.

Participants will engage in discussion sharing their individual experiences with teaming, interpreters and interpreting. Participants will leave with a list of effective strategies, tactics and best practices for DI-HI teaming.

Sign language interpreting in varying cultural and linguistic contexts.

Mark Wheatley
Contact: mark.wheatley@eud.eu

EUD Executive Director

The European Union of the Deaf, a European not-for-profit NGO and the only supranational organization advocating the rights of Deaf sign language users was for the first time presented with a unique interpreting situation at the European Parliament in both Strasbourg and Brussels in autumn 2011. For a lobbying campaign, Deaf people and interpreters from varying countries had to work together to discuss the issue of a Written Declaration regarding the accessibility of 112 emergency services with Members of the European Parliament (MEPs) from all EU Member States. A Deaf lobbyist from one country worked alongside a sign language interpreter (in International Sign) from another country to convince an MEP from yet another country (or occasionally also the same) to sign a Written Declaration (Details can be found here: http://eud.eu/Written_Declaration-i-332.html).

The presentation will draw upon the experiences made during the lobbying period and try to analyse best practice as well as show the new hurdles that the team came across. Examples include cultural differences between the Deaf person and the interpreter but also the interpreter/Deaf person and the MEP. This exceptional situation posed new challenges on the interpreter and the Deaf person, having to adapt not only the language used but also for instance the way one entered the MEPs office depending on the nationality and cultural background of the MEP. An interpreting setting like this requires far more adapting on the interpreter's side than in a usual conference setting for example. Furthermore, significantly more exchange is needed with the Deaf person and a deep cultural knowledge of various cultures and subtleties in the spoken as well as the signed language is expected.

About the contributors

Patricia Brück
patricia.brueck@utanet.at

Patricia Brück got a M.A. Degree for Sign Language Interpreting (EUMASLI) after having completed her interpreting studies for spoken languages in the 1980s (Master of Philosophy). After having worked as a translator, IT trainer, programmer, IT consultant, user interface designer, author of several software manuals, and editor of several publications, she learned Austrian sign language and did her education as a sign language interpreter. She has been working as a professional sign language interpreter for more than 12 years now. Her area of expertise is educational interpreting from secondary level through vocational training to university lectures, conference interpreting and political settings. Her academic interest lie in team interpreting, gender issues in interpreting and the ethics of the profession.

Maartje De Meulder
maartje.demeulder@verbeeld.be

Maartje De Meulder is a PhD researcher at the University of Jyväskylä (Finland) where she is working on a research about Deaf communities' agenda concerning sign language legislation and Sign Language Acts. Before that, she obtained an MSc in Deaf Studies from the University of Bristol and worked as an advocate for the Flemish Deaf Association (Fevlado). She mainly lobbied for sign language education and sign language broadcasting, arguing in favour of Deaf interpreters on television. She is the president of the Flemish Sign Language Centre (VGTC) and co-founder of Tenuto, an organisation offering continued training for VGT interpreters.

Zane Hema
zane@zanehema.com

Zane has been interpreting since 1994 and in 2000 completed a Post Graduate Diploma in BSL/English Interpreting. He also works as an

Interpreter Teacher and Assessor for both vocational and academic programs. He has mentored many interpreters, both students and experienced practitioners supporting their professional development. He is the former National Chair of ASLI, efsli Vice President and WASLI Secretary and continues to support development of sign language interpreting in other countries mostly recently working in the Gambia, Thailand, Nepal and Panama. He was based in London, UK but relocated to Brisbane, Australia at the end of 2012. He enjoys meeting and communicating with Deaf people from around the world believing that such experiences impacts positively on his work. Zane is also a recreational trampoline coach for adults and has a wide range of other disciplines including philosophy, astrophysics and neuroscience. He enjoys reading travel and music.

Isabelle Heyerick

isa@isacorp.be

Isabelle Heyerick is a signed language linguistics researcher, a Flemish Sign Language (VGT) interpreter and a teacher at the interpreter program. She conducts mainly grammatical research for the Flemish Sign Language Centre (VGTC). Her most recent publication is Expressing plurality in Flemish Sign Language (Heyerick & Van Braeckevelt, 2009; Heyerick et al., 2011). Furthermore she is interested in topics such as voice interpreting and back-channel feedback in an interpreted situation. On the first topic she held a presentation with two deaf co-presenters at the 2010 EFSLIT seminar (Finland). She is the co-founder and vice-president of Tenuto, an organisation offering continued training for VGT interpreters. Currently she is enrolled in the Master in interpreting at Lessius University College.

Debra Russell

drussell@ualberta.ca

Debra Russell, Ph.D., COI, is an ASL-English interpreter, interpreter educator and researcher from Canada. Her interpreting practice spans thirty years, and continues to be community based, specializing in legal interpreting. She holds the David Peikoff Chair of Deaf Studies at the University of Alberta. Her teaching has also taken her to locations across several continents. She maintains an active research program, with current projects that focus on Deaf Interpreters, legal interpreting and mediated education settings for Deaf children. She is the author of Interpreting in Legal Contexts: Consecutive and Simultaneous Interpretation and the co-editor of Interpreting in Legal Settings.

Flora Savvalidou

florasavvalidou@yahoo.gr

Flora is a Greek Sign Language Interpreter. She has studied Political Sciences at the University of Athens and has been working as a sign language interpreter since 1997. She holds an MA in Sign Language Interpreting (EUMASLI) and an MA in Special Education (Deaf Education). She has worked in education, in television and in interpreting educational software for deaf students. She is especially interested in the representation taking place in an interpretation and has studied this representation in the specific area of political interpreting.

Risa Shaw

risa.shaw@gallaudet.edu

Risa Shaw, PhD, CSC, CI, SC:L, is Associate Professor at Gallaudet University in the Department of Linguistics. She co-authored curriculum on interpreting in legal settings that is used throughout the US including a fundamentals/ overview course and several specific focus courses (preparation, Deaf/Hearing interpreter teams, monitor role, law enforcement, role and ethics, jury duty, mock deposition). She co-authored the BA curriculum and revised MA curriculum, and contributed to the PhD curriculum in interpretation at Gallaudet. Risa is a highly sought after teacher of interpreters and educators of interpretation and translation, consultant, and interpreter with a specialization in interpreting in legal settings.

Patricia Shores Hermann

pash21@me.com

Patty Shores grew up in the Republic of South Africa, studied in the USA, Canada and the United Kingdom and presently works and resides in Switzerland. She co-directs the bachelor level Swiss German sign language interpreter training program with Prof. Dr. Tobias Haug. She also directs the tertiary Swiss German sign language instructor training program at the Zürich University of Applied Sciences, Special Needs Education (HfH Zürich) and work as a university lecturer.

Ingeborg Skaten

ingeborg.skaten@hib.no

Ingeborg Skaten is a sign language interpreter and sociologist. She has worked within the national deaf association for 20 years. She has been working as a lecturer at the BA programme in sign language interpreting at the Bergen University College (Norway) since 2004. She studies the relationship between the profession of interpreters and consumer societies, where different discourses struggle to define the interpreter, with consequences for the profession.

www.ingramcontent.com/pod-product-compliance
Lightning Source LLC
Chambersburg PA
CBHW061959220426
43662CB00011B/1746